OLD ABERDEEN
Bishops, Burghers and Buildings

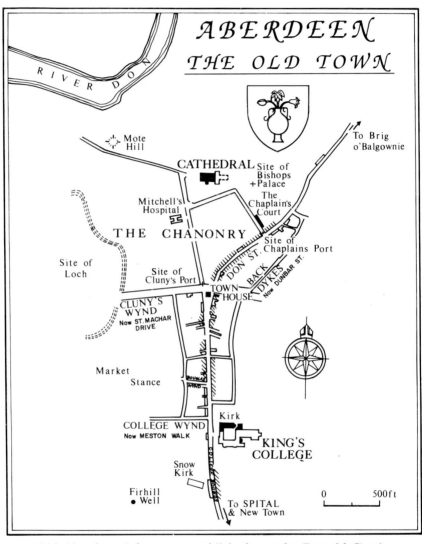

Old Aberdeen (after an unpublished map by Ronald Cant).

Old Aberdeen

Bishops, Burghers and Buildings

edited by
John S Smith

ABERDEEN UNIVERSITY PRESS
Member of Maxwell Macmillan Publishing Corporation

First published 1991
Aberdeen University Press

© Aberdeen University Press for the collected works 1991

British Library Cataloguing in Publication Data

A catalogue record for this book is available from the British Library.

ISBN 0 08 041406 0

Typeset from author generated discs by
Hewer Text Composition Services
Printed by BPCC-AUP Limited

Contents

List of Illustrations   vi

Preface   viii

Introduction
*T. C. Smout, Department of Scottish History, University
of St Andrews*   ix

The Medieval Topography of Old Aberdeen
*Grant G. Simpson, Department of History, University of
Aberdeen*   1

St Machar's Cathedral Through the Ages
*Leslie J. Macfarlane, Department of History, University
of Aberdeen*   14

The Economy and Social Structure of Old Aberdeen in
the Seventeenth Century
*Robert E. Tyson, Department of History, University of
Aberdeen*   38

The College and the Community, 1600–1860
*Colin A. McLaren, Archivist and Keeper of Manuscripts,
University of Aberdeen*   57

Old Aberdeen – the Buildings
*John S. Smith, Department of Geography, University of
Aberdeen*   79

List of Illustrations

Frontispiece: Old Aberdeen (after an unpublished map by Ronald Cant) ii

1. The original site of Old Aberdeen's market-place. 6

2. James Gordon's Map of Old Aberdeen in 1661. 8

3. The Celtic site of St Machar's Cathedral 'where the river curves in the shape of a bishop's crosier'. 15

4. St Machar's Cathedral by 1532 AD. 19

5. The Bishop's Window in St Machar's Cathedral. 22

6. The Western Front of St Machar's Cathedral. 24

7. Bishop Elphinstone watching the building of his University in Old Aberdeen between 1495–1505. 30

8. Location of merchants and chapmen made freemen of Old Aberdeen 1672–94. 46

9. King's College about 1670. 59

10. King's College and the High Street in 1840. 69

11. St Machar's Cathedral showing the Cap Houses on top of the Western Towers and Elphinstone's Steeple. 82

12. Chaplain's Court, The Chanonry. 84

13. The Bede House, Don Street.   86

14. Mitchell's Hospital, The Chanonry.   88

15. The pantiled cottages of Grant's Place.   90

16. The Round Tower, King's College.   92

17. The north west corner of King's College Quadrangle.   94

18. New King's with its protruding staircase bays complete with Gothic tracery.   95

Preface

This is the sixth collection of papers to be published based on the annual local history day conference organised by the Centre for Scottish Studies and the Centre for Continuing Education of the University of Aberdeen. The conference was held on 3 November, 1990 in the Fraser Noble Building, Old Aberdeen. The publication of these papers is particularly appropriate as it coincides with the opening of the Conference and Visitor Centre at King's College. These facilities will increase the number of visitors to the Aulton, all of whom will have a healthy curiosity in, and appreciation of, the historical pedigree of their surroundings. This book should provide the answers to many of their questions. Thanks are due to the authors of the papers for allowing them to be published; to Jim Livingstone and Gordon Stables of the Department of Geography for the photographic illustrations; to Dr Ronald Cant for permission to reproduce his map of Old Aberdeen; to Rod Gunson, the Centre's Conference Organiser, and the staff of the Department of Continuing Education for the publicity and registration duties associated with the conference; to Margaret Croll for producing the final text; and to Professor T.C. Smout, who not only chaired the conference in a firm but friendly manner, but also contributed an introduction to this volume.

John S. Smith
Director of the Centre for Scottish Studies
and Senior Lecturer in Geography
University of Aberdeen

Introduction

T. C. Smout

Scottish urban history has come a long way since Sydney Checkland swept brilliantly but quickly through Glasgow with *The Upas Tree* in 1972 and Ian Adams wrote his broad-brush survey, *The Making of Urban Scotland* in 1978. The nineteenth and twentieth century industrial city, at one end of the spectrum, has been most ably and thoroughly examined from the perspective of its housing history, with some work on its economy and its municipal institutions.[1] At the other end, the medieval and early modern town has been explored anew by archaeologists anxious to record in advance of the bulldozer,[2] and by geographers and historians interested in the processes of building, planning, commerce and handicraft, and in the tensions of urban government.[3] Except in the archaeological studies, however, it has been the big towns of their age that have attracted most of the attention, Glasgow, Edinburgh and Aberdeen in the modern period, Edinburgh, Aberdeen, Perth and other relatively substantial burghs in the earlier age.

Much of what has been most characteristic of Scottish urban society, however, has always been associated with small town life, with the Thrums of Scotland rather than the Dundees. Very little work of quality has been done on the economic and social history of these communities, though the Royal Burgh at Inveraray has been the subject of a fine study, mainly architectural, for the eighteenth century.[4] Particularly unstudied in individual detail have been the ecclesiastical and baronial 'unfree' burghs of the late medieval and early modern centuries, communities enjoying a range of privileges concerning the manufacture and marketing of simple goods for inland sale, but largely excluded until the end of the seventeenth century from the privileges of foreign trade reserved to Royal Burghs.[5] This neglect is unfortunate, as the unfree burghs became extremely numerous – according to one account, 191 were founded between 1450 and 1707, compared to a mere 23 Royal Burghs.[6] Professor Pryde's more thorough study lists 350 '- formal erections', of which 210 were 'viable burghs' of barony and regality and 140 mere 'parchment burghs'. Of the viable burghs 'about 60' allowed their rights to lapse before 1707, but this still left some 160 economically active at the time of the Act of Union.[7]

Such vigorous places were often the subject of the most bitter complaints by their bigger neighbours who felt the encroachment on their prosperity by markets and fairs placed and timed to interfere with their own great occasions of buying and selling. This was particularly obvious in the Convention of Royal Burgh investigation into the condition of their member towns in 1692; on this occasion Aberdeen made a somewhat unstructured and ineffective return, but Brechin, for example, complained bitterly of the laird of Edzell holding a 'weekly marcat on Wednesday and also ane yeirly fair called St Laurence Fair the tyme of the comon fairs of Brechin', as well as about another market held elsewhere in the neighbourhood on Mondays. All these were said to be within three or four miles of Brechin, 'whilkis altogether destroys the touns marcats'.[8] It is plain from Robert Tyson's account below that Aberdeen felt herself similarly threatened by Old Aberdeen, though on this occasion she recorded no formal complaint.

The unfree burghs usually started, and remained, very small, though a few of them, like Greenock, Paisley, Kilmarnock, Falkirk, Leith and Fraserburgh, were destined to grow into sizeable places in the eighteenth and particularly in the nineteenth centuries. Even in the seventeenth century, however, they had a significant role in moulding the character of economic life. Their very numbers imply a familiarity by the Scots with commerce and craftsmanship that contrasted, for example, with the situation in Ireland, where small towns were few and far between, or in Sweden and Poland, both of which attracted hordes of petty merchants and tradesmen from Scotland in the seventeenth century to fill these economic niches. If, in the century 1750–1850, the proportion of the population in towns of over 10,000 grew more rapidly in Scotland than any other European country, it was perhaps in part because of an earlier tradition of urban life in much smaller communities.[9]

It is for these reasons that this study of Old Aberdeen is particularly to be welcomed from the national perspective of Scottish historical studies as well as for its local history interest. The five papers printed here were delivered at a one-day conference of the Centre for Scottish Studies at King's College, Aberdeen, on 3 November 1990, to an audience whose warm appreciation was testimony enough to their importance and relevance locally. Grant Simpson laid the foundations by portraying the geographical features that both made the site attractive and largely determined its bounds, and demonstrated its tripartite division into church centre, market and craft centre, and college centre, all laid onto a framework that nevertheless had strong similarities with other medieval Scottish town plans. Leslie Macfarlane traced the dominant role of St Machar's and its bishops in the fortunes of the settlement in the first few centuries, and then took us through the fascinating history of the Cathedral buildings from the middle ages, through the traumas and decay of the sixteenth, seventeenth and eighteenth centuries, and into the splendid saving and restoration of the nineteenth and twentieth centuries. Robert Tyson's important study of the burgh's economic life and social structure in the seventeenth century showed how, especially after the Restoration, it reached its apogee as a threat to New Aberdeen by the vigour of its markets and the range of its crafts. It probably owed this moment of glory to Scottish (and north-eastern) inland trade which was growing faster than external trade: when the fortune of sea-borne commerce revived strongly again in the eighteenth century the situation was once more reversed. Colin Maclaren vividly portrayed the inter-relationships of student life and town life through the disciplinary proceedings of the kirk session, and the contribution of the faculty to the community. John Smith returned us, finally, to the visible Old Aberdeen of today with illustrations of the wealth of historic buildings in the burgh, from Elphinstone's King's College to the small vernacular houses, from the ancient clerical precincts to the fine private house that the Macleans of Coll built for their student sons.

Reflections on the book may best be left to the reader, but it is impossible for an outsider to come to the University of Aberdeen and not to be struck by the exceptional visual quality, continuity and vitality of Old Aberdeen. It is still, manifestly, the ecclesiastical burgh of the medieval bishops, though the twentieth-century circular road has sheared off the northern section in a most unacceptable way. It is not, admittedly, very visibly the market town and manufacturing centre of the seventeenth century, a public house, bookshop, post office and small store hardly amounting to a significant retailing centre. But that other medieval intention, to endow a university, has so greatly enlarged its original sphere as to encroach on all the remainder of the town and to adapt it for its own purposes; in the process Old Aberdeen has become host to the most interesting university campus in Scotland, by cherishing old buildings and constructing new ones in a maze of interwoven sites. Its beauty, on a sunny November day, is a reminder that old and new can, with sensitivity, be reconciled into a living entity. These papers help us to understand how it came about. Perhaps even more importantly, they help to show us what towns like this have meant to Scotland in the past.

REFERENCES

1. See for example G. Gordon and B. Dicks (ed.), *Scottish Urban History* (1983); G. Gordon (ed.), *Perspectives of the Scottish City* (1985); J. Melling (ed.), *Housing, Social Policy and the State* (1980); M.J. Daunton, *House and Home in the Victorian City: Working-class Housing 1850–1914* (1983); D. Englander, *Landlord and Tenant in Urban Britain 1838–1918* (1983); D. MacCrone and B. Elliott, *Property and Power in a City: the Sociological Significance of Landlordism* (1989); R.G. Rodger (ed.), *Housing in Twentieth-century Scotland* (1989); J.S. Smith and D. Stevenson (eds.), *Aberdeen in the Nineteenth Century: the Making of the Modern City* (1988). The University of Strathclyde is involved in the production of a multi-volume *History of Glasgow*.

2. See especially the series produced from 1977 under the heading of Scottish Burgh Survey by Robert Gourlay, Anne Turner Simpson and Sylvia Stevenson and others, under the title

Historic Arbroath (or some other burgh): *the Archaeological Implications of Development.*

3. M. Lynch, M. Spearman, G. Stell (eds.), *The Scottish Medieval Town* (1988); J.S. Smith (ed.), *New Light on Medieval Aberdeen* (1985); M. Lynch, *The Early Modern Town in Scotland* (1986).

4. I.G. Lindsay and M. Cosh, *Inveraray and the Dukes of Argyll* (1973).

5. There is, however, an excellent edition of *The Court Book of the Burgh of Kirkintilloch, 1658–1694,* published for the Scottish History Society in 1963, with an introduction by G.S. Pryde which gives a very good account of the evolution and functions of the burghs of barony and regality in Scotland.

6. A. Ballard, 'The theory of the Scottish burgh', in *Scottish Historical Review,* Vol.13 (1915), p.22.

7. Pryde, *op. cit.* pp.lxxx, lxxxiii.

8. *Extracts from the Records of the Convention of the Royal Burghs of Scotland, 1677–1711* (1880), p.611.

9. T.M. Devine and R. Mitchison (eds.), *People and Society in Scotland,* Vol.I, *1760–1830* (1988), p.29.

The Medieval Topography of Old Aberdeen

Grant G. Simpson

If we look at Old Aberdeen as it survives at the present day, it is not difficult to see that it is, like a fly in amber, a well preserved example of an old Scottish town surrounded by the environs of a spreading modern city. But it is not quite so easy, at first sight, to appreciate in detail its basic topography – the geographical skeleton which has profoundly influenced the development of the settlement over many centuries. The purpose of the present contribution is to attempt to sketch this fundamental structure and to comment on aspects of its significance in a historical context.

While the estuaries of the Rivers Dee and Don, and their associated valleys, form two definitive elements of the region, the actual landforms, on which and within which human settlement had to proceed, also need our careful attention. As Dr John Smith has expressed the position, 'early historical and medieval Aberdeen developed on a series of fluvioglacial sand and gravel mounds, entirely masking Old Red Sandstone conglomerates'.[1] The land on which Old Aberdeen was created consists of small hills, wandering watercourses, lochs or marshy areas, along with flat, sandy links stretching on the east side of the settlement towards the shore of the North Sea.

The waters and the hills of the area have particularly affected, and at times hindered, the processes of growth. On the north the River Don has over the centuries meandered in different courses across the flat land now known as Seaton Park; and probably created, in the geological past, the bluff immediately to the north of St Machar's Cathedral which physically constituted the northern limit of urban activity. Only about 300 yards to the west of the Town House and market-place, the very heart of the burgh, lay formerly the Loch of Old Aberdeen, a barrier to any westward extension until it was drained in 1662. Its site is now represented by the school playing fields beside the traffic roundabout at the junction of Bedford Road and St Machar Drive. One small but important stream has now almost totally disappeared underground as a result of modern changes. This was the Powis Burn, which ran from the west, was joined by a tributary from the southern shore of the Loch and then proceeded east, through the environs of the present Johnston and Crombie Halls. It still does so, although culverted, and continues to the east, under University Road. Coming under King Street, it goes towards the Links and later changes its name to the Tile Burn. The very name Powis Burn reveals its topographical significance in the area, since the word 'pow' in Scots means a slow-moving stream flowing through flat lands, or, by extension, a watery, marshy place. The Powis Burn created just such a boggy area on either side of College Bounds, where King's College itself and the two halls of residence now exist. The problems so created will emerge at later points in our story.

The hills of Old Aberdeen do not seem formidable to a modern eye, but they were sufficient to act as early barriers. To the west of the Cathedral is the Kettle Hill, along the ridge of which runs the path linking the Botanic Garden to the Arboretum. To the south-east of the Loch lay the Glebe Hill, now crowned on its summit by the Queen Mother Library. At the south end of the burgh was the rather more prominent Spital Hill, across which went the roadway connecting the town to its lively and sometimes dominating 'big brother', New Aberdeen.

Such were the landforms of the area; and within them lay the routeways which were one of the earliest and most vital man-made elements. Historians have all too often given insufficient attention to the early communication lines of Scotland.[2] These routes obviously link places which early travellers were anxious to reach: human decisions lie behind their creation. They may skirt round wet areas or awkward hills, but may equally well strike boldly across these, as College Bounds does up the slope of Spital Hill and as the Gallowgate does at the steep northern entry-way to New Aberdeen. The more distant aiming-points of the transport route which forms the central spine of Old

Aberdeen become entirely obvious if we examine the region. Travelling from the north people wanted to cross the River Don, using the Bridge of Don from at least about 1300, and to make for the ancient and holy site of St Machar's church. Don Street slips past its precincts and turns south to become the High Street of the burgh. In continuing southwards the objective was to reach the Dee Estuary (or more strictly the mouth of the Denburn), where a point of sea access permitted contact with both water transport and trading operations. Trade certainly functioned there from the twelfth century, when New Aberdeen was made a royal burgh, but it is more than likely that the route from the north had been in use long before that. Roads, unfortunately, are difficult to discuss historically: they are infrequently mentioned in early documents and are not usually productive of dateable artefacts. Although the entire length of College Bounds and the High Street has recently been dug up for the purpose of re-laying the setts, no features have been spotted which could have been of help to the historian or the archaeologist.[3]

The main route through Old Aberdeen is therefore readily explicable in terms of the objectives which people had in view. But we must also now narrow the focus and look at the street layout and structure of the town itself. Within the natural landscape man-made features can tell us much about the economic and social requirements of those who decided on the physical form of the town, whether by one particular decision or through evolutionary growth over a long period. In other words, the street patterns and what they contain relate both to the configuration of the ground and to the needs of the community.

Geographical study has identified three fairly standard layouts among the older towns of Scotland.[4] A parallel street pattern, as at Crail, in Fife, for example, indicates some degree of deliberate town planning, and possibly demonstrates a need for expansion resulting from a period of economic prosperity. The convergent style of street plan, well exemplified at Selkirk, reveals a need to focus on some vital area or building, such as the market-place, or a church, and may also be a direct response to the demands of the local topography. New Aberdeen is such a burgh, established on what is physically a very awkward site, within which hills and waters are even more serious constraints than in Old Aberdeen.

But the third form of town plan is both the commonest and the simplest: the single-street pattern. Old Aberdeen has essentially that structure, although the Chanonry, which was a separate precinct, also displays the convergence of two streets towards the Cathedral.

All these plan-forms present certain standard features which can be made to tell us about the thinking of town-planners and urban inhabitants; and Old Aberdeen is in this respect a good example. The crowding of house frontages on the main street is very usual and provides excellent evidence of the fundamentally economic functions of the burgh. Trade was at its core, even in a small burgh such as this. Traders were anxious to reach their customers as directly as possible and the houses of both merchants and craftsmen were frequently built flush with the street, to catch the passing trade. The frontage of each property was narrow (often no more than about 20 feet), because everyone wanted 'a piece of the action'.[5] Even in the early middle ages there are references in Scottish burgh documents to 'booths' or 'windows': an indication that the front part of the burgess's house functioned as his shop. Another regularly recurring element of the plan was a widening of one of the principal thoroughfares to provide space for the open-air market. In Old Aberdeen this was appropriately situated in front of the Town House, where the High Street splits in two, with one route proceeding ahead to Cluny's Port, an entry-gate into the Chanonry, the other curving to the right and going northwards, under the name of Don Street.

The narrowness of the house frontages made it inevitable that the attached ground behind each would take the form of a long strip, known as a rig or croft. In some major burghs, such as St Andrews and Haddington, strips survive even today to the length of 200 yards and more. In Old Aberdeen, a much smaller town, some rigs up to 80 yards remain visible on the ground. The walls at the rig-ends formed a continuous structure which in most Scottish burghs was hardly more than a boundary-line delimiting the inner urban area. Such burgh walls usually had little defensive value. Beyond the walls there often ran outer lanes, now represented to the west of Old Aberdeen by Elphinstone Road, and to the east by Dunbar Street. Further out still lay the burgh fields, in which the inhabitants could pursue cattle grazing and arable cultivation. Their individual crofts permitted the cultivation of garden crops and trees and the keeping of smaller animals, such as pigs. The burgess, accordingly, was essentially a smallholding farmer as well; and the burgh was something integrated with its surrounding countryside and not merely an isolated urban unit.

Physically, then, Old Aberdeen was like many another small Scottish town of medieval origin. What gave it unusual distinction was that it possessed both a cathedral (from about 1130) and a university (from 1495). Only St Andrews and Glasgow were its equivalents in these respects, and both were larger in scale. Although in fact a tiny settlement by English or European standards, it was technically a cathedral city. Constitutionally it was from 1489 a burgh of barony, under the authority of the bishop. The various elements of its life are reflected in its physical form, which can be analysed in greater detail by dividing the town into three sectors.

The oldest and most prestigious area was ecclesiastical: the Chanonry, enclosed within is own walls and centred on the Cathedral. As Dr Leslie Macfarlane discusses St Machar's in detail later in this volume,[6] comment here can be brief. But two points are worth making. The principal inhabitants of the Chanonry before the Reformation were the clergy of the Cathedral; and they too, like the burgesses, had crofts attached to their houses, or manses. These crofts or gardens were extensive – some may originally have been more than one-third of an acre – and their size reflects the social significance of their possessors within the community.[7] Secondly, it can be suggested that parts of the layout of the Chanonry may constitute a very ancient structure of landholding. The four principal officials of the Cathedral chapter were the chancellor, the chantor, the dean and the treasurer, and their manses lay in one line facing the Cathedral itself. The Aberdeen chapter was first established as a formal body about 1240, and it seems a reasonable assumption that the properties attached to these posts would have been designated about that time, or fairly soon thereafter.[8] One minor benefit of that planning process is that these and some other Chanonry properties today possess as soil a beautiful, black, workable tilth: the result of cultivation as garden ground for something like seven hundred years.

1. The original site of Old Aberdeen's market-place.

The next area may be described as the commercial sector, represented by the properties facing the High Street, which ran from the Town House to the lane now called Meston Walk, opposite King's College.[9] As already indicated, this is a standard single-street urban structure. It has a widening for the market-place, in the centre of which there once stood the market cross, now a mere fragment and wrongly sited in an ignominious position at the rear end of the Geography Department. Some additional comments can be made about this area: the trading and manufacturing centre of the town. It need be no surprise that a mercantile community should develop here on the periphery of a very old and much-frequented religious site such as St Machar's, with its own body of clergy and their retainers. In the geographical surroundings which have been described, it is again not unnatural that the town should grow in the form which modern planners refer to as 'ribbon development'. And once again the material evidence will spell out part of the story. The well-known plan-view of both towns of Aberdeen, created by the Rev. James Gordon in 1661, reveals in Old Aberdeen houses crammed on the street-line, but almost no buildings at all erected in the crofts behind. This presents a striking contrast to the building development history of a major burgh such as Edinburgh, where by the early modern period many plots had been largely built on, often to the very ends of the rigs.[10] Edinburgh, as the capital, attracted money and people and possessed a notably active economy. Old Aberdeen functioned at a much more modest level, but even so must have been typical in scale of many of the approximately two hundred and sixty non-royal burghs which existed in the kingdom by the mid-seventeenth century.[11]

To the south of this commercial area lay the educational sector. Study of it immediately raises the question: why is King's College situated where it is? So far as the Chanonry and the High Street areas are concerned, reasons for their locations are readily visible, as has been argued above. However, when bishop William Elphinstone had to decide in 1495 on a position for the buildings of his new university, his choice was in practice rather limited. To the north of the Cathedral the ground fell sharply, and to the east of it lay his own episcopal palace. To the west of the Chanonry and the High Street were the hindrances presented

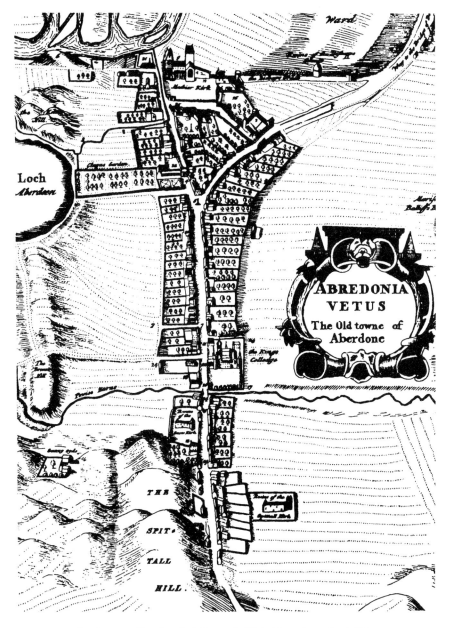

2. James Gordon's Map of Old Aberdeen in 1661.

by various hills and the Loch. At the southern end of the settlement area fairly steep slopes led up to the Spital Hill; and on the east side, beyond the back dykes, were various burgh fields and then the sandy links. It therefore seems fairly certain that the bishop was forced by these realities to look for ground in the south-eastern quadrant of the Old Aberdeen area. But here further problems confronted him, since the Powis Burn, as already described above, had created boggy conditions in that vicinity, which would make it difficult to provide solid foundations for major buildings. Perhaps, however, there was also benefit in this predicament, since such land cannot have been costly to buy. Possibly the bishop was, like a modern developer, 'snapping up a gap site on the cheap'! At any rate, he and his technical advisers effectively solved their difficulty. Parson Gordon, in the commentary attached to his plan-view of 1661, describes the College buildings as they then were and records that 'the foundation of the whole structure, as it rests on yielding and wet soil, was laid on oaken piles at great expense and trouble'.[12] The principle of sinking a wooden raft in a bog to provide support is a very ancient one. The idea worked well here, since the buildings stood firmly, apart from slight subsidence at the east end of the Chapel at some early date.

The buildings of King's College have been often described, but it has not so frequently been pointed out that what Elphinstone and his colleagues created in this area was an enclosed precinct. There was already one in Old Aberdeen: the Chanonry. But the earliest depictions of the College show clearly that its main buildings were surrounded by a wall, which may have been some nine feet high, possibly more.[13] Historians have seldom noted sufficiently the prominence and significance of the enclosure of certain medieval institutions. The monastery is an obvious example: a community intended to be shut off from the world.[14] King's College was never meant to be as exclusive as that: the inhabitants of Old Aberdeen, for example, could attend services in the Chapel and hear sermons provided for them in its nave. But the students in the early days were under enclosed discipline: they required permission to go out of the College, and its gates 'were closed and locked at 8 p.m. in the winter and 10 p.m. in the summer'.[15] Even in Victorian times the College boundary fronting the High Street and the north end of College Bounds was marked by heavy iron railings. High walls and spiked railings are intended to be symbols of separateness. Such features tend to be forgotten, since we have been 'brainwashed' into modern, 'conservationist' ways of thinking, which prefer open sight lines and the removal of obstructions. The men of bishop Elphinstone's generation, therefore, saw a process of major educational development in this part of the burgh. Yet it must also be noted that the College precinct had certain outlying units. The manses of several teachers – the mediciner, the canonist, the humanist and the civilist – all lay facing College Bounds, with their gardens behind.[16] The name 'Humanity Manse' still survives. The University in fact spilled out from behind its walls and possessed properties stretching as far as the northern slope of the Spital Hill.

Yet the story of this part of Old Aberdeen also involves another unusual element, initiated in the late seventeenth century: the establishment of a small country estate in close proximity to the town. In 1691 Alexander Fraser, regent, and later sub-principal and professor of Greek at King's, purchased 12 roods of land, i.e. an extent of about 220 feet, lying almost opposite the College. On account of the activities of the Powis Burn, much of the ground was 'deep sinking mire'.[17] A man of enterprise in business as well as an active academic, he proceeded to drain the area and erect various buildings on it, including Powis Lodge, of which a 1697 wing still survives. Before his death in 1742 he had added other pieces of adjacent property, forming a long, narrow estate, towards the west end of which Powis House was later built, in 1802. A commentator writing about 1724 described the Powis lands opposite the College as 'the only best improved land about the town'.[18]

The fact that the entrance gateway of an estate lay directly on one of the main streets of a burgh was given greater visual prominence when in 1833 Hugh Fraser Leslie of Powis, to whose family the estate had passed in 1773, erected two impressive entrance towers, which still exist.[19] Alexander Fraser had helped to integrate town and country, and his descendant gave strong architectural emphasis to this fact. There may be a few other examples of Scottish estates entered directly from a burgh street, but not many. On the main square of the old burgh of Fochabers, in Moray, lay the entrance to the policies of Gordon

Castle, which was only about 400 yards distant along a driveway. By about 1810 the duke of Gordon had moved the site of the town much further from his front door.[20] About the same period another duke was engaged on similar activities. At Kelso, Roxburghshire, between about 1816 and 1821, the duke of Roxburghe demolished most of the village of Wester Kelso and created in its stead a walled garden and an elaborate estate entrance, which still functions, complete with electrically operated heraldic gates.[21] The whole subject of communication routes between adjacent towns and estates deserves further study.

Much of the topography of Old Aberdeen remains with us. Many quite remarkable changes have occurred within the landscape; but more than merely the skeleton is visible – the street layout, the long rigs, the boundary walls, the ancient churches. If we learn how and where to look, we can find a lot of the past still here in the present.

REFERENCES

1. J. S. Smith, 'The physical site of historical Aberdeen', in J. S. Smith, ed., *New Light on Medieval Aberdeen* (Aberdeen, 1985), 1–9 (at p.1). See also the useful bird's-eye view of the area, ibid., 3.

2. But see Alexander Fenton and Geoffrey Stell, eds., *Loads and Roads in Scotland and Beyond* (Edinburgh, 1984).

3. For some details of a highly organised communal scheme for re-laying the High Street in 1636, see Grant G. Simpson, *Old Aberdeen in the Early Seventeenth Century: a community study* (Aberdeen, 1975), 4.

4. J. W. R. Whitehand and K. Alauddin, 'The town plans of Scotland: some preliminary considerations', *Scottish Geographical Magazine*, 85 (1969), 109–21.

5. See R. M. Spearman, 'The medieval townscape of Perth', in Michael Lynch, Michael Spearman and Geoffrey Stell, eds.,

The Scottish Medieval Town (Edinburgh, 1988), 42–59, esp. 56; and David Murray, *Early Burgh Organization in Scotland* (2 vols., Glasgow, 1924), i, 107, n.2.

6.   Below, pp.14–37.

7.   For a plan of the Chanonry manses and gardens, see A.M. Munro, ed., *Records of Old Aberdeen* (2 vols., New Spalding Club, 1899, 1909), ii, 256.

8.   D. E. R. Watt, *Fasti Ecclesiae Scoticanae Medii Aevi: second draft* (Scottish Record Society, new series, vol.1, 1969), 5–6. There was one further senior official of the diocese, the archdeacon, whose manse lay at a right angle to the four mentioned above, and facing the present entrance lodges of St Machar's churchyard.

9.   St Machar Drive is a modern intrusion, built in 1921–2.

10.   Gordon's plan has been often reproduced: see *Abredoniae Utriusque Descriptio* (Spalding Club, 1842) for the entire work; and Simpson, op.cit., frontispiece, for the Old Aberdeen section. For a similar type of plan-view of Edinburgh in 1647, which demonstrates the built-up character of the rigs, known technically as 'burgage repletion', see T. C. Smout, *History of the Scottish People, 1560–1830* (London, 1969), 48–9.

11.   G. S. Pryde, *The Burghs of Scotland: a critical list* (London, 1965), nos. 82–351.

12.   Arthur Mitchell, ed., *Geographical Collections . . . by Walter Macfarlane* (3 vols., Scottish History Society, 1906–8), ii, 507.

13.   Gordon's plan (see above, n.10) includes a detailed vignette of the buildings. This is also reproduced in David Stevenson, *King's College, Aberdeen, 1560–1641* (Aberdeen, 1990), 121, along with an oil painting (p.3), which is the earliest surviving view of the College. For the latter, see illustration 9, p.59 this volume.

14.   For comment on the importance of the precinct, see Peter Fergusson, '"Porta patens esto": notes on early Cistercian gatehouses in the north of England', in Eric Fernie and Paul

Crossley, eds., *Medieval Architecture and its Intellectual Context* (London, 1990), 47–59, esp. 47–50.

15. L. J. Macfarlane, *William Elphinstone and the Kingdom of Scotland, 1431–1514* (Aberdeen, 1985), 386.

16. For detailed locations, see ibid., 339. 'College Bounds' as a street name appears somewhat odd, since its line continues beyond the western boundary of the College precinct. Perhaps it meant 'the area at, and beyond, the College boundaries'?

17. Details of the history and growth of the Powis Estate are in J. G. Burnett, ed., *Powis Papers, 1507–1894* (Third Spalding Club, 1951), a useful but confusingly edited work. Quotation from p.6.

18. Ibid. The description is that of William Orem, town clerk of Old Aberdeen at the time.

19. Ibid., 366–70.

20. T. R. Slater, 'Parks, gardens and policies: the changing landscape around the castle', in J. S. Smith, ed., *North East Castles: Castles in the landscape of North East Scotland* (Aberdeen, 1990), 32–55, at pp.48–51.

21. Alistair Moffat, *Kelsae: a history of Kelso from earliest times* (Edinburgh, 1985), 162–5.

St Machar's Cathedral Through The Ages

Leslie J. Macfarlane

Many of us will have visited St Machar's Cathedral at some time or other in our lives. We can easily call to mind those fortress-like towers and twin spires; and inside, its rough cast walls, those massive cylindrical columns, and that flat ceiling with those three rows of shields: an austere building, simple but impressive. Many will also be familiar with the famous legend attached to its history – of how St Machar, a companion of St Columba, set out from Iona during the second half of the sixth century to preach the Gospel to the Picts of this area, and built a church on or near where the Cathedral now stands because, according to the legend, he was told to build his church 'where the river curves in the shape of a bishop's crosier just before it enters the sea', which could readily accord with the Cathedral's present site.[1] But, there is much more we can know about the Cathedral and its history than that, and the purpose of this essay is to give an overview, in the light of the latest historical research, on the building itself, on the clergy and ministers who have served both it and the community of Old Aberdeen throughout the centuries, and on the relevance of the Cathedral then and now.

We can deal very briefly with the first five hundred years of the Cathedral's history, or rather, its pre-history between 590–1130 A.D. The truth is that, although many books and learned articles have been written about this early period, some arguing that Christianity reached these parts through the missionary endeavours of Britons led by St Ninian from the south west, and others that it reached us through Celtic missionaries working their way down from Inverness, led by St Machar, we really have no firm written or archaeological evidence to date to prove it either way, as has been clearly shown in an article published by

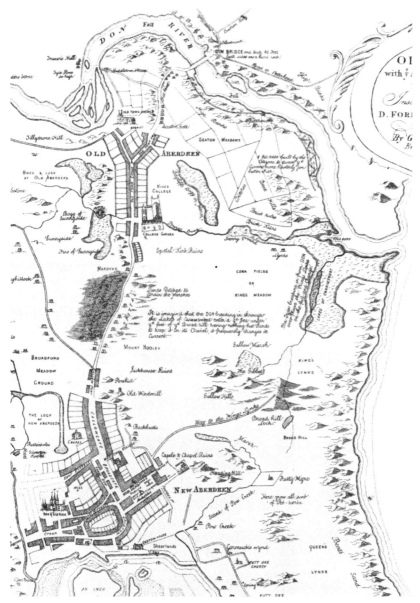

3. The Celtic site of St Machar's Cathedral 'where the river curves in the shape of a bishop's crosier'.

the Friends of St Machar's Cathedral in 1982.[2] So provided we bear in mind that the story about St Machar building his church here on its present site comes to us only through medieval records written eight to nine hundred years after the event,[3] we can keep an open mind on the legend that a church dedicated later to St Machar probably was established here in the late sixth century, and that the only way we could confirm this legend would be if we were able to excavate beneath the present Cathedral and to come across the remains of this early Pictish church. At any rate, until we have evidence to the contrary, we are entitled to accept the view that it was from or near this site on the bank of the Don that the Gospel was first preached to those early Pictish fishing communities huddled around the mouths of both the Don and the Dee, round about the end of the sixth century A.D.

The real history of the Cathedral began, however, when David I reorganised the Scottish church on Continental lines from 1124 onwards, by setting up clear diocesan boundaries, transferring the seat of the ancient diocese of this area from Mortlach in Banffshire to Old Aberdeen in or about 1131, and encouraging bishop Nechtan to build a more permanent stone building where the old Pictish church stood.[4] From then on we are on much firmer historical ground, since written evidence now becomes available in the form of charters showing us the extent of royal and other gifts of land and rents to be held by the Cathedral as free alms in perpetuity. Copies of papal and royal letters also now begin to appear which confirm the Cathedral's earliest privileges, fishing and milling rights, and its exemptions from tolls and taxes. Cathedral registers, too, were now being compiled by its clergy which list the statutes of the Scottish Church defining the proper areas of jurisdiction between the Church and the State as well as the parochial duties of the clergy, while a separate series of registers now begin to list the organisation of the diocese and the stipends of all its clergy.[5] In short, what we are beginning to see, with all this burgeoning of Cathedral records from 1131 onwards, is the gradual absorption of the diocese of Aberdeen into the legal and administrative structure of the western Church as a whole, of which the Scottish Church was now clearly a part. We shall be discussing some of these documents in more detail later; but the reason why we are able to know a good deal about the Cathedral, its bishops and canons, and then its ministers and the community of Old Aberdeen itself, is simply because a useful amount of its medieval records has survived, as have, of course many of its modern records from the Reformation onwards, from which a number of local historians have already given us a lively account of St Machars over the past 850 years.[6]

To turn, first then, to the building itself. The Cathedral we now see is not the one built by bishop Nechtan and his successors in the twelfth century. All that remains of that building is a small flat stone abacus which once adorned the top of one of the slender columns dividing its Norman nave from its aisles. But if we look at similar contemporaneous churches then being built throughout twelfth century Scotland, like Monymusk or Leuchars,[7] we can reasonably deduce that this first Cathedral was Scottish Romanesque at its best: a modest sized building of sandstone with strong exterior walls, rounded windows, a simple but impressive west entrance without a narthex or covered portico, and a light interior culminating in the chancel, possibly with a semicircular apse at the east end. Given the expansion of Cathedral business throughout the thirteenth century, however, which witnessed the introduction of a Cathedral Chapter consisting of some thirteen prebendary canons living in the Chanonry, it is clear that this first Cathedral became too small to accommodate all its activities; for it is evident that it now required a Chapter House where the canons could meet weekly to discuss diocesan affairs, a library for its clergy, and a court where disputes in ecclesiastical law could be heard.

In consequence, at some stage in the 1280s, the then bishop of the diocese, Henry Cheyne, decided that the time had come to build a new and bigger Cathedral. This was clearly going to be a tricky operation since it had to be on the same site, and he simply could not demolish the old Cathedral when it was in daily use. Accordingly he screened off the old nave which was to be kept in use, demolished only the east end of the building and began to build what he intended to be a large and beautiful choir which would form the central crossing of his new Cathedral. He had no sooner positioned the two massive columns which were to form the western pillars of this crossing, however, when Edward I invaded Scotland and bishop Cheyne found himself compromised and forced to accept fealty of the English king, as a result of which Robert I exiled him and the work ground to a halt. Letters in the Vatican Archives show that bishop Cheyne's successor, Alexander Kininmund I appealed to pope Clement VI in 1344 to allow him to raise funds to continue the building,[8] but this was a period of severe political disorder when English ships anchored off Aberdeen and the City was burnt and looted, so little could have been done to encourage progress for some years. How much of the new nave had been marked out by this time we have no means of knowing. But we have clear evidence that the work was able to be taken firmly in hand some eleven years later when Alexander Kininmund II became bishop of Aberdeen in 1355, for it was he who demolished what he could of the old Cathedral while still allowing it to remain operable, and then spaced out and began to build the massive cylindrical columns of the present nave, marked out and partially built the Cathedral's external walls, and then went on to construct the two fortress like towers at the west end; and all this during his episcopate between 1355–1380.[9]

With the return of James I from his captivity in England in 1424, a period of comparative peace followed in the North East, which allowed successive bishops of Aberdeen to press ahead and try to complete the Cathedral. And here the work of Henry Lichton, its bishop from 1422 to 1440 was decisive. It was he who completed the nave and the aisles up to the roof, who completed the western front between Alexander Kininmund's towers, built the north transept (where he was buried), and began the central tower over the crossing.[10] His successor Ingram de Lindsay roofed the nave of the Cathedral between 1441 and 1458, paved the floor with flagstones, fitted the doors, glazed the windows, decorated the interior walls and brought the building into use.[11] The choir and central tower were then roofed, and the building of the south transept begun. His successor Thomas Spens (1458–80) furnished the choir with its stalls,[12] but it was left to bishop Elphinstone to build a beautiful steeple over the central tower, to lead the roof of the nave, to continue the south transept, and to plan an enlarged choir and Lady Chapel to the east of the central crossing.[13] His successor Gavin Dunbar added the twin spires at the Cathedral's west end to give balance to Elphinstone's central spire, he furnished the

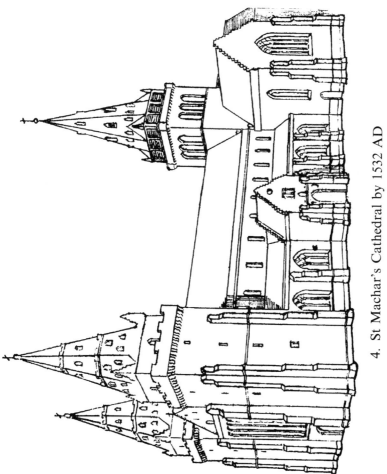

4. St Machar's Cathedral by 1532 AD

nave with a handsome ceiling, completed the south transept (where he was buried), and he may well have completed the Lady Chapel to the east, thus giving the building the cruciform structure by about 1532 which Henry Cheyne had planned in the 1280s.[14] So at last, after a prolonged disastrous war with the English, raids and sporadic attacks, and many other set backs, the building was complete. It had taken two hundred and fifty years, but it was undoubtedly one of Scotland's finest Cathedrals, reflecting all that was best in the Aberdeen character and its craftsmanship: a mostly granite structure, somewhat architecturally conservative with its Romanesque west front, massive cylindrical interior columns, and rounded clerestory windows above the aisles, but strongly compact and able to resist the harsh winter storms which so often assailed the North East.

But worst storms were ahead. Within thirty years, the Reformation had brought its adherents up from the south and with it, their determination to rid Old Aberdeen of all signs of its medieval past. In 1560 the Cathedral was stormed by reformers who were prevented from wrecking it by the timely arrival of the earl of Huntly and his troops. In 1568, however, the earl of Moray gave orders to strip the lead from the roof of the Cathedral. This was duly carried out by an Edinburgh burgess, one William Birnie, together with the removal of the massive peal of bells from the central tower, the Aberdonians refusing to take part in its desecration.[15] But en route for Holland, where the lead and bells were to be sold, Birnie's overloaded ship sank with all hands, including William Birnie, just outside the harbour at Girdleness. The Cathedral then became the Reformed religion's parish church, but being underfunded and stripped of its medieval benefactions, its ministers could not afford its upkeep, so that the building became partially ruinous, and in 1688 the central tower collapsed, bringing down and crushing at the same time the north and south transepts and the gabled-up east end. Before then, in 1640, the visiting Covenanters had already vandalised many of the Cathedral's interior reminders of the ancient religion – crucifixes, statues of the saints and the like, but astonishingly they left Dunbar's beautiful ceiling alone, although it bore pope Leo X's coat of arms and the heraldic shields of all the medieval Scottish bishops, – perhaps because they could not reach it; or that too, would have been destroyed.

It would be out of place at this point to discuss the struggle between the episcopalian and presbyterian forms of church government which raged throughout seventeenth century Scotland, but the final establishment of presbyterianism in 1691 did affect the interior layout of St Machar's Cathedral (now of course no longer a Cathedral) in that the central position of the *word* rather than the *sacrament* in the presbyterian form of worship gave pride of place to the pulpit rather than to the table or altar; hence the most privileged wealthier worshippers at the Cathedral began to build elaborate private desks or boxes and then lofts or galleries orientated towards the pulpit in order to establish their status; to be followed quickly by the Incorporated Trades lofts, leaving the floor of the kirk to humbler folk, women and children. Thus, everybody now had their place, not only in society, but especially in church. In short, in David Stevenson's memorable phrase: 'the reformed church had banished the visual arts from churches like St Machar's where the arts had once been employed to glorify God, but then allowed them back again on the strict condition that they were only used to glorify men'.[16] In fairness it must be added that from the early seventeenth century onwards, the Kirk Session and the Town Council of Old Aberdeen had taken over the care of the fabric of the building, and throughout the seventeenth and eighteenth centuries had patched up the roof, glazed a number of windows in the north and south aisles, planted trees in the kirkyard and repaired its dykes, had maintained the Cathedral clock and given it a new dial, and had built a substantial gallery at the west end.[17] But it is clear from the nineteenth century Kirk Session minutes and from those of the Town Council that the cost of maintaining the fabric could only be sustained by continued appeals to the Church's central funds, the Ministry of Works and private benefactors. The Gothic revival throughout Britain, however, with its renewed interest in medieval architecture and ecclesiastical arts and crafts, gave impetus to those in the North East who longed to renovate what was left of the Cathedral even if they could not restore it to its former glory. Accordingly, by the 1870s, with much public spirit, though not without much heartsearching and fierce controversy, all the

5. The Bishop's Window in St Machar's Cathedral.

desks and lofts in the nave were swept away, the interior walls were stripped of plaster and repointed, Dunbar's ceiling was cleaned and repainted, five stained glass windows by Cottier replaced plain ones around the deambulatory or free space behind the altar at the east end, the London firm of Clayton and Bell installed the large stained glass west window, and a massive plain glass window was inserted into the eastern gable end.

The latter part of the nineteenth century and the first half of the twentieth century saw further interior improvements: a new heating system, a new organ, and especially the installation of eight further stained glass windows, three of them in the south aisle, the Crombie window showing the arrival of St Machar and his monk companions, the Bishops' window showing the Cathedral's master builders Kininmund, Lichton and Elphinstone, and the War Memorial window, all being designed by Dr Douglas Strachan, who had an exceptionally sensitive understanding of the medieval use of colour and of the relation of his windows to the position of the sun at various times in the day. The other five windows, all of them in the North Aisle, were much more traditional and were designed by Marjory Kemp and Margaret Chilton. And in 1953 William Wilson solved the problem of making a satisfactory focus of the Cathedral's east end by inserting three beautiful stained glass lancet windows into this large stone mass, which allowed the Crucifixion and other biblical scenes he depicted, to flow across the strong vertical stone mullions and thus give the whole window an exceptionally fine unity.[18]

A generous donation from the McRobert Trust in 1968 gave further encouragement to those who were not only responsible for the fabric of the Cathedral but also appreciative of its long history, and in consequence the room above the south porch was converted into a Charter Room where many of the Cathedral's ancient as well as modern records are now displayed. A little later, the Friends of St Machar's Cathedral were founded, who have since been able to raise the funds to embellish the Mitchell Chapel, remodel the pulpit, assist in the cleaning of the organ, and to help in the resiting of the baptismal font.

In bringing to a conclusion this section on the building itself, fitting tribute must be paid to all those generous benefactors who raised over half a million pounds in the 1980s to carry out a

6. The Western Front of St Machar's Cathedral.

massive restoration of the Cathedral's entire exterior fabric, to clean, repair and repaint Dunbar's ceiling, to re-site the font, to reconstruct and enlarge the west end, and to instal a fine peal of bells in the south west tower to replace those removed by William Birnie in 1568.[19] Thus both the interior and the exterior of the present building are in good shape to enter the twenty-first century, despite the many changes they have witnessed in the past five hundred and fifty years.

But let us now turn to those monks, priests and ministers who have served both the church and the community of Old Aberdeen for 1400 years. If we examine the legends of those Celtic and British saints associated with Deeside and Donside in Dark Age Scotland, it is clear that monks like Machar, Devenick, Drostan and Moluag were literate, widely travelled – some having already been on pilgrimage to Rome – and that besides preaching the Gospel they looked after the sick, comforted the dying, and introduced the Christian form of burial to the native Picts. Moreover, given that similar Culdee communities elsewhere in Scotland, like Kinrimund at St Andrews,[20] took in orphans and young persons dedicated to the religious life, it is more than likely that the monks had already established a school at St Machar's by the tenth century, if not long before, for the instruction of the young, as well as a hospice for guests and for the sick. Theirs was a hard life of total commitment. It was they who not only laid the foundations of the Christian faith in our area, but also the beginnings of community care, both in New and Old Aberdeen, and our debt to them is incalculable.

The Gregorian reformation of the secular clergy in eleventh century Europe, however, together with the reforms initiated by St Margaret and her royal sons, brought to an end the predominantly monastic and Culdeian structure of the Scottish Church, and from the early twelfth century onwards, as we have already briefly indicated, the Scottish Church entered the administrative framework of the Western Church with its firm provincial, diocesan and parochial structures and its adherence to a universal canon law. As far as the medieval diocese of Aberdeen was concerned, its boundaries now took in the whole of Aberdeenshire and Banffshire less Strathbogie, plus a small area in Kincardineshire, consisting of some eighty-five parishes (later to grow to one hundred) grouped within the five deaneries of Aberdeen, Mar, Buchan, Boyne and Garioch, with St Machar's Cathedral at the heart of this network.[21] Its bishops were, as always, responsible for the moral and spiritual welfare of the whole diocese, but since, with the rest of the Scottish bishops, they were now among the king's chief counsellors, and therefore often required to be with the king, it was soon evident that they would need a small team of clergy at St Machar's to conduct the affairs of the diocese in their absence. By 1157 bishop Edward had received authority from the English pope Adrian IV to institute canons at the Cathedral,[22] and by the 1230s they are a recognisable team with specific duties: the dean, to take the bishop's place at the weekly meetings of the Chapter where diocesan problems were discussed; the precentor or chanter who was responsible for the liturgy at the Cathedral – to look after the choir, arrange the music for the services and to take charge of the 'sang' school; the treasurer, whose duty it was to oversee the lighting and heating of the Cathedral, to be responsible for all the furnishings and vestments, and to maintain a constant supply of oil and wine for the daily services; the chancellor, who looked after the bishop's and the Chapter's correspondence with popes, kings and others, besides being responsible for the Cathedral grammar school; the archdeacon who watched over the problems and difficulties of all the parish priests throughout the diocese, and who spent much of his time crossing and crisscrossing the whole area and reporting back to the Chapter at regular intervals; and the official of the diocese, the bishop's chief legal officer, who held court in the north west tower of the Cathedral four or five days a week throughout the year to hear and settle disputes concerning marriage, legitimation, testamentary debts, property, contracts, moral misdemeanours, and much other business which would now be heard in burgh and sheriff courts and the Court of Session.

By the 1230s, too, additional canons were required to oversee the management and the finances of the bishop's and the Chapter lands, namely those lands which had been gifted to St Machar's since the eleventh century. Just how extensive these were can be gleaned from one of the Cathedral's earliest charters which lists the benefactions made by Malcolm III, David I and

Malcolm IV as 'the whole vill of Old Aberdeen, half the waters
of the River Don, Sclattie, Goval, Murcar, Kinmundy, the tenth
of the royal tax on ships coming into Aberdeen, of the corn
there, the king's tenth of the burgh of Aberdeen itself, a tenth of
the royal dues between the Dee and the Spey, the vills of Clatt,
Tullynessle and Rayne and the church of Daviot'.[23] When one
examines the ninety-five charter entries which follow, and takes
into account the fact that all these lands, fishings and other
rights were leased out or feufermed, we begin to see how steadily
the Cathedral grew in wealth, and why it eventually needed not
only the twenty-eight canons it had by 1445, but also a whole
team of procurators, lawyers, surveyors, bailies and clerks to
keep an eye on its income, collect its rents and watch for
dilapidations of its property. By 1511 the rentals alone on the
bishop's and Chapter's lands amounted to £682.17s.8d.,[24] so that
by the Reformation in 1560, the Cathedral's income in cash and
kind must have amounted to well over £1000 per annum, a very
large sum indeed in those days.

What did the Church do with all this money? First there was
the upkeep of the twenty vicars choral, the chaplains and the
choir boys, who sang the Divine Office daily in the Cathedral on
behalf of the whole community. Next came the care of widows,
orphans, the destitute and the sick, a constant obligation the
Church was pledged to maintain; then there were the educational
needs of the diocese, chiefly the maintenance of the boys and
young men aspiring to the priesthood, and those being trained at
the Cathedral grammar school. There was also the cost of law
suits, mostly over disputes concerning Church lands; there was
papal taxation, and of course, the upkeep of the Cathedral fabric
and the heavy cost of its building programme. Whether the
Cathedral Chapter was wise to have burdened itself with all this
pressing expenditure is simply an academic question; they were a
part of an ecclesiastical system common throughout the western
Church, which in itself merely reflected the social and economic
pattern of feudal Europe in the later Middle Ages. And one has
to remember that it also provided employment and inspiration
to generations of stonecutters and masons, joiners, stained glass
craftsmen and artists of all kinds, and that the majority of people
saw the beautiful Cathedral which their generosity had created,
as a valid and worthy expression of their faith and devotion.

But before we leave this medieval clerical enclave centred around St Machar's, with its canons, vicars choral, choir boys, grammar school boys and chaplains, all living in the Chanonry and going about their daily tasks, we ought to pause for a moment and think of the bishops of Aberdeen who lived among them; for it is clear from those registers which have survived that these were the men who really changed the character of Old Aberdeen itself. From the late thirteenth century onwards they were almost without exception university graduates. And although, whether they liked it or not, much of their time was spent on the king's business, either in Council or on Parliamentary Committees, or as ambassadors to foreign countries, few of them ever forgot their obligations to their diocese, or the social conscience required of them. As early as the 1170s we find bishop Matthew founding St Peter's hospital on the Spital, from which it derives its name today;[25] Hugh de Benham in the 1270s encouraged the earl of Buchan to found an almshouse at Turriff;[26] and bishop Gavin Dunbar founded an old folk's home for twelve old men just outside the west end of St Machar's Cathedral in 1532.[27] These bishops also cultivated good relations with the royal burgh of Aberdeen, giving over a portion of their fishing rights of the Dee to them, supporting the costs of the building of their parish church of St Nicholas, and one of them, bishop Elphinstone, built the handsome stone bridge over the Dee for them which is still much in use today. But the greatest change they brought about was in Old Aberdeen. For quite apart from their continued support in building the two successive cathedrals here, one of them, William Elphinstone won over James IV to create Old Aberdeen into a burgh of barony in 1489,[28] which gave its inhabitants the right to hold a weekly market on Mondays under their own Mercat Cross, besides two major fairs a year, and most important of all, authority to elect their own magistrates and other officials needed to control the affairs of the burgh, thus no longer making Old Aberdeen economically and politically dependent on the royal burgh of Aberdeen – an identity they were to preserve for the next four hundred years. Then in 1495 Elphinstone gave his most lasting gift to his newly founded Burgh by creating in its midst Scotland's third University, an event which not only profoundly changed the social and economic life of Old Aberdeen, but which also transformed it into the intellectual centre of the North, which it happily remains to this day, especially when one considers its contribution to the area over the centuries in the fields of medicine, forestry, agriculture, fishing, and now, in oil related disciplines and business studies.

It is difficult from the evidence of the sources, however, to avoid the conclusion that the period from the Reformation to the nineteenth century was one of steady and inevitable decline for the Cathedral and the Burgh of Old Aberdeen. For a start, after 1560 most of the Church's wealth was diverted elsewhere, a number of its lands being feued to lay heritors or converted into hereditary temporal lordships which, if it enriched local lairds and the aristocracy, certainly impoverished the stipends of the new ministers and left precious little to maintain its sadly ravaged fabric.[29] In addition, the Burgh itself now had to face burdens which had once been borne by the church: a Burgh school and the stipend of a qualified master to run it, and the obligation to look after the poor of the parish. Indeed, a study of the Kirk Session records and those of the Burgh shows only too clearly how difficult both authorities found it to meet these and other obligations imposed upon them in a radically changed and much less protected world.[30] The Kirk Session records of the seventeenth and eighteenth centuries especially make bleak reading and seem to be obsessed with Church collections and fines and penalties for moral misdemeanours, although this has to be seen against the background of the church's basic financial instability and the fact that the civil actions which had once been pursued in the Cathedral's Consistory Court were now dealt with in the Commissary Court, leaving only charges against the moral law to be the Kirk Session's responsibility. Moreover, throughout these difficult centuries both the Kirk Session and the Town Council had to come to terms with the oscillating political and religious interests of both the Crown and King's College. As for the former, Scottish kings had taken it under their protection and defended its privileges, however formally, since the eleventh century, as we have seen; and many examples could be given to show how monarchs even after the Reformation, whether Stewart, Dutch, or Hanoverian, upheld their rights on appeal, but provided always that they were

7. Bishop Elphinstone watching the building of his University in
Old Aberdeen between 1495–1505.

assured of the Kirk's loyalty; and as for the latter, the patronage of King's College was often a mixed blessing in that a Covenanter Principal like Dr Guild in the 1640s could and did wreak havoc on Cathedral property. Nevertheless, the appointments of other Principals, sub-principals and regents of the College as Ministers of the First Charge at the Cathedral did much to maintain the level of preaching throughout the seventeenth and eighteenth centuries, and to bind more closely the ties of the Cathedral with the Burgh and the College, given that the same men were almost invariably on the Town Council and saw the community, including their own College, as one. But what really counted in these matters was obedience to the Crown. Given that from the Kirk, the College and the Burgh, the Crown could afford to let them run their own affairs. To step out of line as all three were tempted to in 1715 and again in 1745 could be disastrous, and was briefly for all three in those years; and understandably, given their long-held Stewart and episcopalian sympathies. It is not surprising to find, therefore, that after 1745 they kept their heads down and concentrated more on their own local problems.

It is not possible in so brief an essay to discuss the lives and work of even a few of the ministers who have served St Machar's since the Reformation, although the Kirk Session and other records bring vividly to life many of their struggles, difficulties and discouragements, revealing only too well the political and religious upheavals of their age. Moreover, we have to remember that even after 1560 the Cathedral parish covered a wide area well beyond Kirkton of Seaton, so that in the early days it must have been quite beyond the work of one minister to serve, and this situation was not remedied until 1648 when two ministers were appointed. What does come through the records is that on the whole these ministers doggedly administered to their flocks, baptising, preaching, visiting the sick and burying the dead. The reversion to a sole charge in 1928 still left the minister with a parish of some 20,000, a problem which was only relieved in the late 1980s with the creation from it of a new parish St Columba's, at the Bridge of Don, leaving St Machar's today with some 1400 residents.[31]

What place, then, can be found for St Machar's Cathedral in the modern world of today? What function has it left to fulfil?

These are sensitive questions. Doubtless a large number of the many thousands of tourists who visit it annually from all over the world, must see it, as they see so many of our cathedrals, simply as a part of our ecclesiastical heritage – museums, almost, which they believe the State might be better persuaded to upkeep, given the large sums of money required to maintain and restore their fabric. But we who live and work here believe otherwise. For we are aware only too clearly of the rich role it plays in the religious, cultural and social life of the Aulton, the City and the North East. Religiously, it shares a positive ecumenical programme of services with the other two denominational cathedrals in the City, and this in addition to the quiet but essential parochial work required of its minister. Culturally, as Aberdonians know so well, it annually provides inspiring musical concerts, recitals and plays. Socially, it still binds the Aulton together, for we have only to ask ourselves what would Old Aberdeen ever have been without it? Without its long tradition as a Christian focal point over the past fourteen hundred years, would the village ever have survived? For certainly we would have not been established as a proper burgh capable of running its own affairs had not one of its bishops petitioned the king so to erect it as a personal favour; an event whose five hundredth anniversary we were happy to celebrate last year.[32] Nor indeed would we have had a University here in our midst without that same bishop's perspicacity and vision. But most of all we know the real purpose of our Cathedral. For it is not only, as it always has been, a supportive presence to the poor and those in need of spiritual comfort, but it remains the centre of a worshipping community, ever mindful of the words of the Psalmist: 'O Lord I have loved the beauty of your house, the place where your glory dwells'.[33]

REFERENCES

1. The legend stems from the life of St Columba written by Adomnan (627–704), abbot of Iona, for which see *Adomnan's Life of Columba*, edd A. O. and M. O. Anderson (Edinburgh 1961); and see also the *Acta Sanctorum, Junii II* for Columba

(Paris 1867), 179–233, and the *Registrum Episcopatus Aberdonensis [REA]* I, ed C. Innes (Edinburgh 1845), x.

2. J. D. Galbraith, *St Machar's Cathedral: The Celtic Antecedents* (Aberdeen 1982).

3. Especially from *Legends of the Saints in Scotland in the Dialect of the Fourteenth Century* II ed W. M. Metcalfe (-Edinburgh 1896), lines 769–775, in pages 1–46; III, pages 308–18, esp. 309; and in the early sixteenth century *Breviarium Aberdonense, pars estiva*, ed W. Blew (London 1854), where the legend is included in the ninth historical lesson for the feast of St Machar on 12 November, which runs on fol. clvii^r: Ubi Flumen praesulis instar intrat mare, baculi Mauricius [Macharius] cepit habitare (Where the river in the shape of a bishop's crook enters the sea, there Machar chose to dwell).

4. *REA* I, xviii–xix; II, 246–47; *Fasti Ecclesiae Scoticanae Medii Aevi*, comp. D. E. R. Watt (St Andrews 1969), 1; G. Donaldson, 'Scottish Bishops' Sees before the reign of David I', *Proceedings of the Society of Antiquaries of Scotland* 87 (1955), 106–17.

5. L. J. Macfarlane, *St Machar's Cathedral, Aberdeen and its Medieval Records* (Aberdeen 1987). Many of these records have been printed in *REA* vols I and II (Edinburgh 1845).

6. The twelve Occasional Papers published by the Friends of St Machar's Cathedral are listed at the end of this chapter.

7. F. and P. Sharratt, *Écosse Romane* (Edinburgh 1985), 178–82, 349–50; D. MacGibbon and T. Ross, *The Ecclesiastical Architecture of Scotland*, I (Edinburgh 1896), 215–18, 309–14.

8. *REA* I, 131–33.

9. H. Boece, *Murthlacensium et Aberdonensium Episcoporum Vitae*, ed J. Moir (Aberdeen 1894), 24; L.J. Macfarlane, 'Who Built the Western Towers of St Machar's Cathedral?', *Friends of St Machar's Cathedral Annual Report, 1985*.

10. Boece, *Vitae*, 31–34; R.G. Cant, *The Building of St Machar's*

Cathedral (Aberdeen 1976) 5–6; W. Kelly, 'Description of St Machar's Cathedral', in *Logan's Collections*, ed J. Cruickshank (Aberdeen 1941), 154–55.

11. Boece, *Vitae*, 34–37.

12. *ibid.*, 53.

13. R.G. Cant, *The Building of St Machar's Cathedral*, 6–7.

14. *ibid.*, 7–10.

15. David Stevenson, *St Machar's Cathedral and the Reformation, 1560–1690* (Aberdeen 1981), 1–5; the same author, *King's College Aberdeen 1560–1641* (Aberdeen 1990), 8.

16. *ibid.*, *St Machar's Cathedral . . .*, 15.

17. *ibid.*, 14–15; G.G. Simpson, *Old Aberdeen in the early Seventeenth Century* (Aberdeen 1980), 3; Agnes Short, *The Kirkyard of St Machar's Cathedral* (Aberdeen 1982), 2–4; the same author, *Old Aberdeen in the Eighteenth Century* (Aberdeen 1985), 6–7.

18. Crear McCartney, *The Stained Glass Windows of St Machar's Cathedral, Aberdeen* (Aberdeen 1979).

19. A.S. Todd, 'Restoration and Renewal', *Friends of St Machar's Cathedral Annual Report, 1986*; L.J. Macfarlane, 'The Bells of St Machar's Cathedral', *Friends of St Machar's Cathedral Annual Report 1987*.

20. M.O. Anderson, 'The Celtic Church in Kinrimund', *Innes Review* XXV (1974), 67–76.

21. L.J. Macfarlane, *William Elphinstone and the Kingdom of Scotland 1431–1514* (Aberdeen 1985), 200 and back-end map; I.B. Cowan, *The Parishes of Medieval Scotland* (Edinburgh 1967).

22. Robert Somerville, *Scotia Pontificia* (Oxford 1982), 45–47; *REA* I, 5–7.

23. The first four charters printed in *REA* I, 3–8, from one of which this extract has been taken, have now been shown to be spurious, for which see G. W. S. Barrow, *Regesta Regum Scottorum* I (Edinburgh 1960), 181, 258–59, but their substance may have been more reliably transmitted in the more carefully worded bull of confirmation in 1359, for which see Robert Somerville above, 46.

24. *REA* I, 379.

25. *REA* I, 11–12; I. B. Cowan, D. E. Easson and R. N. Hadcock, *Medieval Religious Houses: Scotland*, 2nd ed (London 1976), 163.

26. *REA* I, 30–34; I. B. Cowan above, 168.

27. *REA* I, 401–06; I. B. Cowan above, 163.

28. *The Register of the Great Seal of Scotland 1424–1513*, ed J. B. Paul (Edinburgh 1882), 401; *Records of Old Aberdeen* I, ed A. M. Munro (Aberdeen 1899), 5–12.

29. For example, all the lands, rents, fermes and dues which had once belonged to the vicars choral and chaplains of the Cathedral were granted to Alexander Hay, the Director of Chancery, on 9 May 1573, *Register of the Privy Seal of Scotland*, VI, 370–71.

30. *Records of Old Aberdeen* II, ed A. M. Munro (Aberdeen 1909), 1–194; I (Aberdeen 1899), 32–204.

31. A. S. Todd, 'The Role of St Machar's Cathedral in the Present and in the Future', *Friends of St Machar's Cathedral Annual Report, 1987*.

32. With the Community Play 'Elphinstone', and St Luke's Fair, 10–14 October 1989; but see also L. J. Macfarlane and Agnes Short, *The Burgh and Cathedral of Old Aberdeen, 1489–1989* (Aberdeen 1989).

33. Psalm 26, v.8.

A USEFUL READING LIST FOR THE CHAPTER ON ST MACHAR'S CATHEDRAL

Occasional papers published by the Friends of St Machar's Cathedral

No.1   Leslie J. Macfarlane, *St Machar's Cathedral in the Later Middle Ages* (1979).

No.2   David McRoberts, *The Heraldic Ceiling of St Machar's Cathedral* (1981).

No.3   Grant G. Simpson, *Old Aberdeen in the Early Seventeenth Century* (1980).

No.4   Ronald G. Cant, *The Building of St Machar's Cathedral, Aberdeen* (1976).

No.5   Crear McCartney, *The Stained Glass Windows of St Machar's Cathedral* (1979).

No.6   Ian B. Cowan, *St Machar's Cathedral in the Early Middle Ages* (1980).

No.7   David Stevenson, *St Machar's Cathedral and the Reformation 1560–1690* (1981).

No.8   J. D. Galbraith, *St Machar's Cathedral: the Celtic Antecedents* (1982).

No.9   Agnes Short, *The Kirkyard of St Machar's Cathedral, Aberdeen* (1982).

No.10   Agnes Short, *Old Aberdeen in the Eighteenth Century* (1985).

No.11   Leslie J. Macfarlane, *St Machar's Cathedral, Aberdeen, and its Medieval Records* (1987).

No.12   Leslie J. Macfarlane and Agnes Short, *The Burgh and Cathedral of Old Aberdeen, 1489–1989* (1989).

See also:
> M. R. Sefton, 'The Soldier Ministers of Old Machar', *Friends of St Machar's Cathedral Annual Report* 1990.
>
> Stewart Todd, *The Cathedral Church of St Machar, Old Aberdeen* (Aberdeen 1988).

All these publications may be obtained from The Secretary, St Machar's Cathedral, The Chanonry, Old Aberdeen AB2 1RQ

The Economy and Social Structure of Old Aberdeen in the Seventeenth Century

Robert Tyson

Most descriptions of Old Aberdeen written in the eighteenth century dealt overwhelmingly with the Cathedral and King's College while its proximity to New Aberdeen has led many historians since that time to treat it as an integral part of that city or, worse still, to ignore it altogether.[1] And yet until 1891 Old Aberdeen was a separate burgh with its own distinct institutions. It was also second in size to New Aberdeen among the towns of Aberdeenshire until towards the end of the eighteenth century, when it was finally overtaken by Peterhead,[2] and for much of the seventeenth century had a lively and growing economy. The purpose of this essay is to examine the economy and social structure of the Aulton during the latter century and to explain why its growth appeared such a threat to the citizens of its much larger neighbour.

The earliest documentary evidence that we have of the economy is James VI's charter of 1489 which created it a burgh of barony. This gave the inhabitants:

> . . . full power and liberty to buy and sell within the said burgh, wines, wax cloth, woollen and linen, broad and narrow, and other merchandise; and to have and to hold bakers, brewers, butchers and sellers of flesh and fish, and other craftsmen in any way belonging to the freedom of the burgh of barony.[3]

They were also allowed to hold a weekly market on Mondays and two public fairs a year, one on Skyre Thursday (the day before Good Friday) and the other on St Luke the Evangelist's Day (18 October) and the following eight days.[4] However, the inhabitants were forbidden to trade overseas or to retail foreign (i.e. staple) commodities. These privileges were reserved to the royal burgh of New Aberdeen which had a monopoly of all trade within the liberty or sheriffdom of Aberdeen. As James Gordon put it in 1660, all other towns, villages and hamlets within Aberdeenshire 'are bound to engage in commerce by the sea and land at the pleasure and with the permission of the citizens of Aberdeen, and it is unlawful for them to trade otherwise'[5]. Burghs of barony like Old Aberdeen were supposed to be small enclaves whose trade and industry served local needs. Because of this limited economic role, they were taxed only as part of the sheriffdom whereas New Aberdeen had to pay its share of the 'cess' or taxation levied upon the royal burghs.[6]

The relationship between New and Old Aberdeen can only be understood in the light of the former's determination to defend its privileges and the latter's attempts to infringe them. Other burghs of barony in the shire tried to do likewise but Old Aberdeen became a particular worry because it was so near New Aberdeen and lay astride the road to the Brig O' Don, which was 'the most special brig and passage quhairby the hail vivaris [victuals] and fewal cummis to this town, out of Buchan, Gareauch and utheris pairtis thairabout'.[7] Moreover, whenever disputes arose between the two, the bishop of Aberdeen, the lairds and gentlemen who lived there, and the professors and regents of King's College were able to provide strong leadership and protection.

The economic and social structure of Old Aberdeen can be seen for the first time in the list of inhabitants which was made in May 1636. It was probably compiled to allow an inquest or jury of thirty of the oldest and most respectable citizens to identify:

> . . . all infamous persones all ydleris, and those that hes no certaine calling to live be and wer not provided of kaill and fewall and other necessaries of good neighbourheid and upon receptaris of begeris ydleris and vagabounds and strangeris without licence.[8]

The inquest found forty such persons. Some were expelled by the burgh and the remainder had to find cautioners for their future conduct or were set to work as servants. This was a period of high food prices and the expulsions were probably an

attempt to relieve pressure on the limited resources of Old
Aberdeen.[9]

There were 831 people on the list who lived in 202 households,
giving a mean household size of 4.1. There is no way of knowing
how many inhabitants were left out but the two most prominent
citizens, bishop Adam Bellenden and provost Sir Alexander
Gordon of Cluny, are both missing as are the twelve bedesmen
of Bishop Dunbar's Hospital, the students of King's College,
and some of their teachers. If these are included, Old Aberdeen
at that time probably had a population of c.900 compared with
c.9,000 in New Aberdeen.

Of the 202 heads of households, 151 were male. At the top of
the social pyramid were five lairds and gentlemen, who probably
lived in the former canons' houses in the Chanonry, and twelve
professional men. The latter group consisted of six lawyers
(including Thomas Davidson, Commissary – Clerk of Aberdeenshire), four professors and regents of King's College, the
minister of Old Machar, and the master of the Music School.
Because of their large families and numerous servants, the
households of these two groups contained 114 people, or nearly
fourteen per cent of the population.

The great majority of household heads, however, earned their
livelihood by manual labour. As in all burghs, there was a
sizeable number who worked on the land. The list gives the
names of fourteen farmers and gardeners but it is likely that
some at least of the thirty-four men who were not given
occupations were engaged in agriculture in some way or other
while a number of tradesmen and even professional men, among
them a regent of King's College, rented crofts adjacent to the
burgh. Other occupations included salmon fishers, servants at
King's College, the town's bellman but only two merchants and
a hawker.[10]

The economy of Old Aberdeen, however, was dominated by
the seventy-five tradesmen, most of whom were members of the
Incorporated Trades. When the trades received their charter
from the bishop of Aberdeen in 1637, there were six of them i.e.
the hammermen (who included cappers and glovers as well as
wrights, coopers and metalworkers), weavers, cordiners or
shoemakers, fleshers, and baxters or bakers.[11] They were in
existence long before 1637 (the hammermen's coat of arms had

the date 1600 painted on it) and there may have been more since in 1609 the burgh council asked nine visitors or deacons to give an account of the money in their hands (unfortunately the names of their trades were not given).[12] The most numerous occupational group were the twenty-two weavers and they were also the richest for in the same year their incorporated trade agreed to give 10 merks (£6.13s.4d.) annually towards the salary of the master of the Music School, twice as much as any other trade.[13] Next in number were the seventeen leather workers, including eleven shoemakers, and they were followed by eleven men involved in the preparation of food and drink (see Tables 1 and 2).

These figures underestimate the numbers actually engaged in manufacturing. The members of this group employed thirty-five male servants (David Abell, deacon of the weavers' trade, had no fewer than seven of them) who presumably assisted as apprentices or workmen, and they may well have received further help from their wives, children and twenty-seven female servants. Moreover, some of the fifty-one female heads of households were also involved in manufacturing. The list unusually gives the occupations of twenty-six of them, most of whom were probably widows. No fewer than fourteen of the twenty-six were connected with the preparation of food and drink (seven breadsellers, three brewers, two sellers of kaill, one of dill, and a 'puddinwricht') and ten with textiles (six spinners, two shankers or stocking-knitters, a tailoress and an embroiderer). The remaining two were a candlemaker and a midwife. Old Aberdeen occasionally enrolled women on its register of trade burgesses; three were admitted in 1617 and a further nine between 1640 and 1677.[14] Of the twenty-five women whose occupations are not given, three were the widows of lairds and others were described as poor or having no means of support.

A further complication is that it was quite usual to have several occupations though the list only gives one for each person. The extent of the problem can be seen in the case of breadsellers. Seven were listed in 1636, all of them women, but in 1643 no fewer than nineteen had to pay fees or entry fines to the bakers trade, of whom only four were women. One was Marjorie Carll who was also described as a breadseller in 1636 but she had been admitted to the burgess roll in 1640 as a huxter or seller of

TABLE 1   OCCUPATIONAL STRUCTURE OF MALE HEADS OF
HOUSEHOLDS IN OLD ABERDEEN, 1636 AND 1695, AND
NEW ABERDEEN 1695 (Percentages in brackets)

Category	Old Aberdeen 1636		Old Aberdeen 1695		Aberdeen 1695	
1. Lairds and gentlemen	5	(3.3)	9	(3.4)	15	(2.2)
2. Professions	12	(7.9)	13	(4.9)	48	(7.2)
3. Agriculture	14	(9.3)	9	(3.4)	33	(4.9)
4. Merchants	3	(2.0)	36	(13.7)	194	(29.0)
5. Tradesmen	75	(49.7)	138	(52.5)	187	(28.0)
6. Other occupations	8	(5.3)	12	(4.6)	49	(7.3)
7. No occupation given	34	(22.5)	46	(17.5)	143	(21.4)
	151	(100.0)	263	(100.0)	669	(100.0)

Source: A. M Munro (ed), *Records of Old Aberdeen* (Aberdeen 1899), 1, 347–55; J. Stewart (ed), *List of pollable persons within the shire of Aberdeen, 1696* (Aberdeen, 1844), ii, 570, 575, 583–632.

TABLE 2   CLASSIFICATION OF TRADESMEN IN OLD ABERDEEN,
1636 AND 1695, AND NEW ABERDEEN, 1695 (Percentages in
brackets)

Classification	Old Aberdeen 1636		Old Aberdeen 1695		Aberdeen 1695	
Textiles	24	(32.0)	31	(22.5)	39	(20.9)
Clothing	10	(13.3)	23	(16.7)	32	(17.1)
Leather	17	(22.7)	43	(31.1)	29	(15.5)
Metalwork	5	(6.7)	9	(6.5)	19	(10.2)
Wood and construction	8	(10.7)	18	(13.0)	47	(25.1)
Food and drink	11	(14.7)	14	(10.1)	21	(11.2)
	75	(100.0)	138	(100.0)	187	(100.0)

Source: As for Table 1

chickens and eggs. Where it has been possible to find other occupations for the fifteen male breadsellers, two were also cordiners, three weavers, one was a smith, and another tilled a croft.[15] Incidentally, only seven of the nineteen appear in the 1636 list, three of them women.

The largest single occupational group, however, consisted of servants living in households, most probably aged between fifteen and twenty-five since it was usual on marriage to leave service. In all there were 96 male and 159 female servants who together made up 19.1 per cent of the population and served in 43.1 per cent of households. These are considerably higher percentages than the 13.4 and 28.5 respectively in a sample of one hundred English communities.[16] The difference may be explained by the relatively large numbers of lairds, gentlemen, members of the professions, and tradesmen living there and by the fact that the North East was a poor region with a large population so that servants were plentiful and cheap.

It is doubtful if Old Aberdeen, unlike Fraserburgh and Peterhead to the north, was a source of much concern to New Aberdeen before 1640. Its handful of merchants offered no threat to the c.350 merchants in the royal burgh, whose trade and population were growing rapidly.[17] Moreover, for its size New Aberdeen had relatively few tradesmen (only 123 were taxed in 1623) and may have relied upon Old Aberdeen for some of its manufactures.[18] During these years the citizens of Old Aberdeen were allowed to use the Stocket forest in New Aberdeen's freedom lands for fuel and pasture, though they had no legal right,[19] and some were admitted freemen of the royal burgh.

The outbreak of the Civil War, however, marked the beginning of a difficult time for the North East generally but particularly for New Aberdeen. It was repeatedly occupied by rival armies who extorted free quarters and supplies while in 1644 Montrose's troops killed 160 of its citizens and sacked the burgh. New Aberdeen claimed that its losses during the war amounted to £1,582,910 Scots but this included a number of ships sunk by bad weather. The amended total of £617,938 Scots, however, was still an enormous sum, the equivalent of over twice the annual rental of the shire. Trade was badly disrupted and it was claimed that exports of plaiding (a coarse cloth made from carded wool) collapsed completely for a time. Fearful of further attacks and unable to earn a living, many citizens fled abroad or to other parts of Scotland. Further depopulation came with an outbreak of bubonic plague in 1647 which killed 1,600 in New Aberdeen (probably about a quarter of the population) and a further 120 in Footdee and Torry.[20] The parish of Old Machar, which included Old Aberdeen, lost only twenty and although the Aulton also suffered from the consequences of war, particularly the quartering of troops, and the removal of the Bishop in 1638, it escaped lightly when compared with New Aberdeen. Its kirk session even provided some relief for those in New Aberdeen who had suffered at the hands of Montrose's troops and during the 1650s its citizens went *en masse* to help with the harbour works.[21]

Although there was some recovery of foreign trade after 1650, it is unlikely that New Aberdeen's exports regained the level of 1639 during the remainder of the century.[22] It was also saddled with enormous debts which had to be paid off with heavy excise duties and still stood at £120,000 Scots in 1695.[23] These difficulties made New Aberdeen much less attractive to the immigrants needed to maintain its population size so that by 1695 it probably had not more than c.7,500 inhabitants compared with c.9,000 in 1640.[24] They also coincided with increasing criticism of the privileges of the royal burghs and a massive increase in the numbers of burghs of barony and non-burghal markets and fairs throughout Scotland. In Aberdeenshire twelve new burghs of barony were created between 1650 and 1707 compared with only two in the first half of the seventeenth century while twenty-nine other places were allowed to hold markets and fairs.[25] Apart from the new creation of Old Meldrum, the main threat to New Aberdeen came from Fraserburgh, Peterhead and a now aggressive and dynamic Old Aberdeen.

Old Aberdeen's challenge, which brought an end to the reasonably good relations with New Aberdeen, opened innocuously in May 1661 with an Act of Parliament ratifying its rights and privileges (to which New Aberdeen objected).[26] In the following March the magistrates instructed the quarter-masters responsible for looking after the three divisions of the burgh, to regulate the stands of the Skyre Thursday fair. Cattle and sheep were to be sold on the hill near Brig O'Don, horses between there and the town, linen and woollen cloth and stockings at the market cross, timber between Cluny's Port and the Loch Wynd, and all other commodities between Cluny's Port and the cross. Similar regulations were drawn up in October 1663 for St Luke's Fair which lasted longer and was concentrated between the Cathedral Manse and King's College on both sides of the street and by the Loch of Old Aberdeen.

Each quarter was to provide six armed men 'for the better keeping of things in good order' while duties were levied on all goods sold there and the rent of each stall fixed at 3s.4d.[27] William Orem in his description of Old Aberdeen in 1724–25 claimed that both fairs 'in popish times stood within the Chanry [sic] and were great ones. But at the beginning of the Reformation of religion, they decayed, by reason of the troubles of the time'.[28] The bishop, reinstated in 1662 following the Restoration, and magistrates were clearly intent on returning the fairs to their former importance and probably succeeded. By 1677 there were so many cloth sellers thronging about the market cross that they impeded traffic and were moved to a more spacious site.[29] Finally in July 1662 the magistrates also obtained an Act of Parliament allowing them to change the weekly market day from Monday to Thursday. Meal, wheat, malt, butter, cheese and other commodities had to be weighed at the Weigh-House (built in 1640) before being sold.[30]

The most startling consequence of these changes was a remarkable expansion in the number of merchants living in Old Aberdeen. Whereas in 1636 there were only two merchants and a hawker, in 1680 it was stated that they were 'now become more numerous than heretofore and by the blessing of God in a better condition than formerly'.[31] In that year thirty-seven of them formed a Merchant Society and were allowed a loft in the Cathedral.[32] Moreover, between 1672 and 1694 no fewer than nineteen merchants and twenty-nine chapmen living outside the parish of Old Machar were admitted as freemen on payment of £20 each. The majority, as might be expected, came from parishes immediately to the north, notably Belhelvie with fifteen merchants and chapmen, Foveran with six and New Machar with five, but some came from much further away, including eight from Kincardineshire, one from Glasgow and another from Jedburgh (see illustration 8 overleaf).[33]

The best indication, however, of how Old Aberdeen had altered since 1636 can be seen in the *List of pollable persons within the shire of Aberdeen* which was compiled in 1695.[34] Compared with 1636, there was little change in the numbers of lairds, gentlemen, professional men and farmers, but there were now thirty-five merchants and 138 tradesmen (see Table 1). The increase in the latter was particularly marked in the case of leather workers who

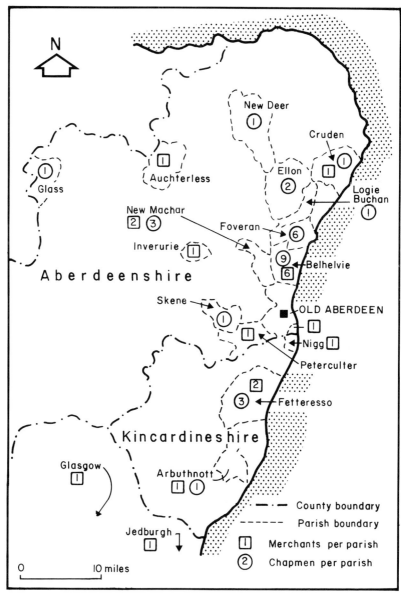

8. Location of merchants and chapmen made freemen of Old
Aberdeen 1672–94.

had risen from seventeen to forty-three between the two dates (see Table 2). The list is probably less accurate for the remainder of the population and is therefore not strictly comparable with the one for 1636. However, it does indicate a population in 1695 of over 1,800, about double that in 1636, and perhaps the largest total in the history of the burgh. If correct, it means that New Aberdeen was now only four times as large.

The poll list for New Aberdeen is much less reliable because of massive tax evasion. It is probable that only half of those who should have paid the tax did so and some of those missing were merchants and tradesmen. For example, it gives the names of five brewers, though we know that c.300 were ruined by the bad harvest of 1695, and only one baker. If we exclude those tradesmen involved in the preparation of food and drink, there were 166 compared with 124 in Old Aberdeen (see Table 2). Although the difference between the two was undoubtedly much greater, there had been a narrowing since 1636. The list also gives the names of 194 merchants (again an underestimate since there were probably at least 250). Although this figure dwarfs the thirty-five in Old Aberdeen, the latter had, as we have seen, large numbers of non-resident merchants and chapmen who were free to trade there while Orem states that between 'the time of Oliver's usurpation' (i.e. the 1650s) and 1720 tradesmen there had the privilege of 'merchandising and malting'.[35] Old Aberdeen was clearly much more of a threat than before 1640, particularly in view of the great difficulties that New Aberdeen was experiencing, and the years from 1660 onwards were ones of almost constant friction.

Each burgh supported its tradesmen against competition from the other. In 1662 Thomas Mitchell and John Ross of New Aberdeen commissioned Alexander Charles, a wright of the royal burgh, to make equipment for one of their malting barns in Old Aberdeen. When William Reid, one of Charles's workmen, came to install it, he was attacked by a mob led by three of the magistrates and armed with guns, pistols, swords and sticks. Despite his protests that he was a freeman of New Aberdeen, his tools were taken away from him.[36] Again, in 1671 the magistrates of Old Aberdeen ordered that no yarn should be sent to New Aberdeen or the countryside but should be reserved for the town's own weavers.[37] New Aberdeen in its turn was concerned about 'the great prejudice our traidsmen susteines by the Spittel and other contrie men working upon their liberities'.[38] An Act of 1592 had prohibited all crafts in the suburbs of royal burghs, generally defined as the area within a mile of the market cross.[39] The Spital, which came within that distance, had sixteen tradesmen in 1636 and no fewer than thirty in 1695, including seventeen shoemakers and five weavers. It is debatable whether the southern boundary of Old Aberdeen ended at the former Leper House (which would include the Spital) or at the Powis Burn. In 1699 the magistrates argued that the freedom did include the Spital but the commissioners for regulating trade between the royal burghs and burgh of barony insisted that it did not and taxed it separately. The Spital, in fact, was the property of the Moirs of Stoneywood and it is perhaps significant that only eight of the thirty tradesmen there in 1695 were freemen of Old Aberdeen.[40] The Act of 1592 was impossible to enforce and in no way hindered the Spital's growth. Indeed its expansion south led New Aberdeen to complain about its 'incroachments upon the bounds of the freedom of this burghe'.[41]

New Aberdeen's main concern, however, was to defend its trade. Old Aberdeen's decision to change its market day from Monday to Thursday, the day before New Aberdeen's, was seen as a particular threat since 'all sorts of merchandise, meill, wheat and other graine coming to the mercate are forstallit and regratit'.[42] Most of New Aberdeen's food requirements and cloth and stockings for export came from the area to the north of Old Aberdeen (i.e. the territorial divisions of Formartine, Garioch and Buchan) and its magistrates were clearly anxious that the Old Aberdeen merchants should not intercept them (forestalling) with the intention of reselling in New Aberdeen at a profit (regrating). They also objected to Old Aberdeen's Weigh House 'which is destructive to the Burgh of Aberdein being ane Burghe Royall and the old toune at most but one burghe of baronie'.[43] The result was an Act of Parliament ordering Old Aberdeen to move its market day to Tuesday and remitting the problem of the Weigh House to the Privy Council. The Act, however, did not state what penalties would be incurred if Old Aberdeen refused to change and was ignored.[44]

New Aberdeen's response was to take the dispute to the Court of Session in Edinburgh where it dragged on for over a decade at considerable expense but with no success.[45] Equally unsuccessful was the attempt in 1668 to prevent seventeen prominent Old Aberdeen merchants and tradesmen (several of whom were freemen of New Aberdeen) from trading in 'wooll, hyds, leather, victuall, cloth . . . stockenes, spyces, hemp, lint, picktarr and uthers steppel goods in hurt and prejudice of the said burgh of Aberdeen liberties'.[46] Old Aberdeen, however, had powerful supporters in Parliament, most notably the Bishop of Aberdeen, and with the advice of the staff of King's College was clearly intent on resisting any attack on its rights. Its magistrates even argued that because Old Aberdeen was a university town, James VI's charter could be interpreted as allowing its merchants to trade in foreign commodities.[47] They were almost certainly wrong but so powerful were the Aulton's supporters in Parliament that New Aberdeen's own agent in Edinburgh was unwilling to proceed in the prosecution. He pointed out that there was growing hostility in Parliament towards the attempts of the royal burghs to preserve their monopoly of trade while Sir George Mackenzie, a leading lawyer of the period, declared that their privileges, 'far from being advantageous either to the public or to private persons' divided Scotland into two unequal parts. Moreover, many of the nobility and lairds in Parliament had recently founded burghs of barony on their lands and had a vested interest in curtailing the privileges of the royal burghs. The result of this opposition was the Act of 1672 which allowed burghs of barony to export their own commodities, import all goods except wine, wax, silk, spices, and woad and other materials for dyeing, 'and sell in retaill all commodities whatsoever'.[48]

Relations between the two burghs continued to be difficult even after 1672. No Old Aberdeen merchant or tradesman was made a freeman of New Aberdeen between then and 1686[49] and Old Aberdeen was caught up in the consequences of New Aberdeen's decision in 1680 to prohibit the import of ground malt. The magistrates there argued that this would improve the quality of the malt used for brewing and bring to the town's mills dues that had previously gone to local landowners. However, it can also be viewed as an act of retaliation against the 'unfree' burghs and their proprietors, including Old Aberdeen, who sold ground malt and forced up prices in New Aberdeen. The latter's magistrates attempted to secure the support of the New Aberdeen craft guilds by offering a number of privileges, including reduced entry fees to the freedom of the burgh, easier admission for their sons, and the right to complain to the magistrates about work of poor quality brought into the town by strangers. Most of the traders accepted these privileges in return for agreeing to the unground malt market but Alexander Idle, deacon of the hammermen, supported the landowners. Because of 'factious and seditious expressions' against the burgesses of New Aberdeen, he was fined £100 and deprived of the freedom of the burgh but in May 1681 was made a freeman of Old Aberdeen 'gratis'. The dispute over the unground malt market dragged on until 1694 when the Court of Session found against the royal burgh.[50]

Relations between the two burghs may have improved towards the end of the 1680s. No fewer than eight Old Aberdeen merchants were admitted to the merchant guild of New Aberdeen between 1686 and 1691 while in 1688 the bishop ordered that 'for eviteing of animosities and troubles betwixt the trades of Old Ab. and trades of New Ab', no tradesman in Old Aberdeen should raise an action against one in New Aberdeen without the consent of himself and the magistrates.[51]

Nevertheless, New Aberdeen still had its grievances. During the 1690s Parliament proposed that the burghs of barony should be taxed. This coincided with a period of acute famine in New Aberdeen (which may have reduced the population by as much as a fifth) and of a severe depression in overseas trade. Moreover, its finances were in an appalling state; in 1691, for example, income was £3,748 Scots but expenditure £11,578, and the magistrates could justifiably claim that the municipal debt 'in a short tyme will swell soe high that the toune will be utterly ruined'.[52] It was therefore not sympathetic when Old Aberdeen in 1699 objected to paying three shillings of every £10 levied on the burghs of barony. The magistrates there claimed that the Old Aberdeen merchants had an extensive trade, 'espeatlie considering that they live within a myle of the Burgh of Aberdeen and have interest in the shipping thereof and have a vast trade of stockings, fingring (a coarse light cloth made from combed wool) and plaiding and intercept the most pairt of these goods when coming to the said Burgh of Aberdeen and import and export all staple products',[53] despite the re-imposition of the royal burghs' monopoly in 1690. Old Aberdeen offered only one shilling on the grounds that it was impoverished by 'quartering [of soldiers] and other public calamaties',[54] of which the most serious was the famine; although less serious than in New Aberdeen, it probably caused a ten per cent fall in the population. The magistrates pleaded that the inhabitants were reduced to poverty, apart from six or seven merchants of whom only one traded abroad. He was James Knight, a freeman of New Aberdeen since 1686, who had a twelfth share in a small ship 'and is most severely taxed by the said Toun year far beyond his trade'.[55] Old Aberdeen's contribution was eventually fixed at two shillings, which meant a payment of £683.14s. James Moir of Stoneywood offered two pence for the Spital and his lands in Old Machar and Newhill 'which he declared he did for preventing their being joyned to the Old Toun of Aberdeen, or under their jurisdiction within the whole freedome or community they were never were . . . [and] he declared ther neither wes at present nor ever befor any merchant residing upon the saids lands that traded or dealt in merchandising'. [56] The offer was accepted.

Of the other major burghs of barony, Fraserburgh's magistrates objected to an initial assessment of four shillings on the grounds that 'our Toun is both depauperat by thir bad years and depopulat and our shipping is quyt lost'. New Aberdeen, however, claimed that its trade in 1699 was £122,000 and that it had 'three pairts of four of shipping as the Toun of Aberdeen hes'.[57] The commissioners inclined towards Fraserburgh's version and reduced its assessment to 1s.8d. Peterhead was to pay 1s.2d., despite New Aberdeen's claim that it had a large number of ships and a thriving trade with Norway and elsewhere and Old Meldrum 9d., 'the said toun having no foreign trade since 1697'.[58] Turriff was also finally assessed at 9d. and Stonehaven in Kincardineshire 10d.[59] By contrast New Aberdeen's contribution in 1697 was £4.10s., though this was well down on the £8 paid before the outbreak of the Civil War, which gives some indication of its relative decline.

The difference in size between the contributions of New and Old Aberdeen underestimates the latter's importance, particularly as regards inland trade. It is likely, however, that its challenge was coming to an end. There had been no increase in the number of merchants there since 1680 and a marked falling off after 1694 of merchants and chapmen from outside becoming freemen. Old Meldrum, fifteen miles to the north-west, may also have usurped some of its functions for although created a burgh of barony in 1671, it already had sixteen merchants by 1695 and a considerable trade in cloth and stockings which were sold to the merchants of New Aberdeen.[60] Moreover, with the final removal of its bishop in 1689 and the transfer of his commissary court to New Aberdeen, it became less attractive to lairds, gentlemen and lawyers.[61]

When Thomas Pennant visited Old Aberdeen in 1769, he called it a poor town while Francis Douglas wrote in 1780 that 'it is now of little account but as the seat of King's College'.[62] Its population in 1790, when we have the first accurate figure, was only 1,713 compared with 20,167 in New Aberdeen and its suburb of Gilcomston.[63] This stagnation or even decline since 1695, however, was fairly typical since only Huntly and Peterhead among the burghs of Aberdeenshire grew significantly during the eighteenth century.

In retrospect it seems likely that Old Aberdeen's growth between 1636 and 1695 and its challenge from 1660 onwards were linked to the difficult problems that New Aberdeen faced during these years and which made it vulnerable, particularly as Parliament was unwilling to uphold its privileges. During the eighteenth century these problems disappeared. Its finances were put in good order and although exports of plaiding and fingrams collapsed completely, these were more than made good by an expansion in the exports of stockings. Like cloth, these were made in the countryside but eventually under the "putting out" system whereby the New Aberdeen merchant-hosiers dealt directly with the producer instead, as with cloth, of buying from them at markets and fairs.[64] This may help to explain the relative decline of many Aberdeenshire burghs, including Old Aberdeen, in the eighteenth century. In addition to experiencing a revival of its foreign trade, New Aberdeen became a major manufacturing centre in its own right, particularly of factory-made textiles. By the end of the eighteenth century it dominated the North East more than ever and only on the periphery of Aberdeenshire were towns sufficiently distant to flourish. Old Aberdeen was now too near for its own good.

REFERENCES

1. See for example William Orem, *A description of the Chanonry, Cathedral and King's College of Old Aberdeen in the years 1724 and 1725* (Aberdeen, 1791), Thomas Pennant, *A tour of Scotland MDCCLXIX* (Chester, 1771), 116–119, and Francis Douglas, *A General Description of the East Coast of Scotland* (Aberdeen, 1826), 148–82 (Douglas's visit was in 1780).

2. Sir John Sinclair, *The Statistical Account of Scotland, 1791–95* [OSA] (rev.ed. Wakefield, 1975–8), XV, 388–89.

3. A. M. Munro (ed), *Records of Old Aberdeen* (Aberdeen, 1899), i, 9.

4. Munro, *Records*, 6–12.

5. James Gordon, *A Topographical Description of Both Towns of Aberdeen,* in *Macfarlane's Geographical Collection* (Scottish History Society, 1907), ii, 492–93.

6. For the privileges of royal burghs and burghs of barony see W. M. Mackenzie, *The Scottish Burgh* (Edinburgh, 1949) 66–82 and T. C. Smout, *A History of the Scottish People* (London, 1969), 157–59.

7. J. Stuart (ed), *Extracts from the Burgh Records of Aberdeen 1570–1625* (Spalding Club, Aberdeen, 1848), 268.

8. Munro, *Records*, 61.

9. Munro, *Records*, 60–62.

10. Munro, *Records*, 347–55. For an analysis of the list and discussion of its background see R. E. Tyson, 'Household size and structure in a Scottish burgh: Old Aberdeen in 1636', *Local Population Studies*, No.40. Spring 1988, 46–54.

11. Munro, *Records*, 301–3.

12. Munro, *Records*, 46.

13. Munro, *Records*, 64.

14. Munro, *Records*, 231–37 (*Register of Merchant and Trade Burgesses*).

15. Munro, *Records*, 73.

16. P. Laslett (ed.) *Household and family in past time* (Cambridge, 1972), 152.

17. D. Macniven, 'Merchants and traders in early seventeenth century Aberdeen' in D. Stevenson (ed.) *From Lairds to Louns* (Aberdeen, 1986), 57–69.

18. M. Lynch, 'Introduction: Scottish towns 1500–1700' in M. Lynch (ed.) *The   early modern town in Scotland* (London, 1987), 13.

19. L. B. Taylor, *Aberdeen Council Letters 1552–1681* (Oxford, 1942–61), ii. 77–79.

20. For Aberdeen in the Civil War see D. Stevenson, 'The burghs and the Scottish revolution' in Lynch, *Early modern town*, 180–86.

21. Munro, *Records*, 91.

22. R. E. Tyson, 'The rise and fall of manufacturing in rural Aberdeenshire' in J. S. Smith and D. Stevenson (eds.), *Fermfolk and fisherfolk* (Aberdeen, 1989, 64–65).

23. Aberdeen District Archives, Letters Supplementary, 1, 1615–1759, No.39.

24. R. E. Tyson, 'The population of Aberdeenshire, 1695–1755: a new approach', *Northern Scotland*, vi. (1985), 125.

25. G. S. Pryde, *The burghs of Scotland* (Glasgow, 1965), 63–80; J. D. Marwick, *List of markets and fairs now and formerly held in Scotland* (London, 1890), *passim*; I. A. Whyte; 'The growth of periodic market centres in Scotland 1600–1707', *Scottish Geographical Magazine*, 95 (1979), 13–26.

26. Munro, *Records*, 21; Taylor, *Letters*, iv, 144.

27. Munro, *Records*, 99–100, 104–105, 106, 109, 124.

28. Orem, *The Chanonry etc*, 114.

29. Munro, *Records*, 128.

30. Munro, *Records*, 23.

31. Munro, *Records*, 294.

32. Munro, *Records*, 294–6.

33. Munro, *Records*, 236–45.

34. J. Stewart (ed), *List of pollable persons within the shire of Aberdeen, 1696* (2 Vols. Aberdeen, 1844); for a discussion of this source see Tyson, "Population of Aberdeenshire", 113–31.

35. Orem, *The Chanonry etc*, 118–19; Munro, *Records*, 179–81.

36. *Records of Privy Council of Scotland*, 3rd series: (Edinburgh 1908), 299–300.

37. Munro, *Records*, 122.

38. Taylor, *Letters*, v, 29.

39. Mackenzie, *Scottish burghs*, 73–74.

40. Munro, *Records*, 386–90.

41. Taylor, *Letters*, vi, 27.

42. Taylor, *Letters*, iv, 221.

43. Taylor, *Letters*, iv, 221.

44. Munro, *Records*, 23–24.

45. Taylor, *Letters*, iv and v, *passim*.

46. Taylor, *Letters*, iv, 373.

47. Taylor, *Letters*, v, 190.

48. Taylor, *Letters*, v.433–39; Mackenzie, *Scottish burghs*, 46–47; T. Pagan, *The Convention of the royal burghs of Scotland* (Glasgow, 1926), 134.

49. *Miscellany of the New Spalding Club* (Aberdeen, 1907), ii, 436–58.

50. Taylor, *Letters*, vi, *passim* but particularly 235–38 (see also Taylor's Introduction, xix–xxii).

51. Munro, *Records*, 144.

52. J. D. Marwick (ed), *Records of the Convention of the Royal burghs of Scotland, 1677–1711*, (Edinburgh 1880), 574–76.

53. Munro, *Records*, 387–88.

54. Munro, *Records*, 390.

55. Munro, *Records*, 388.

56. *Acts of the Parliaments of Scotland*, x (1696–1700) Appendix, 145.

57. *Acts*, Appendix, 144.

58. Acts, Appendix, 144.

59. *Records of the Convention*, 236–37, 361, 381.

60. *Acts*, Appendix, 144.

61. D. Stevenson, *St Machar Cathedral and the Reformation 1560–1690*, Friends of St Machar Cathedral Occasional Paper, No.7 (Aberdeen, 1981), 16–17.

62. Pennant, *Tour*, 116; Douglas, *General Description*, 148.

63. *OSA*, I 117, XIV, 285–86.

64. Tyson, 'Manufacturing', 66–8.

The College and the Community, 1600–1860

Colin A. McLaren

The constitution of King's College, laid down by bishop Elphinstone in his charters of 1505 and 1514, secluded its students as much as possible from the distracting influence of the town.[1] A century later, little had changed. Students attended services in St Machar's on Sundays, they went to the Links for games, and some ate and slept outside the walls; but their comings and goings were rigorously controlled, and they remained, essentially, a body apart.[2] When they did mingle with the community, they were rebuked from the highest quarter: Charles I complained, after his visit to Scotland in 1633, that staff and students of both colleges sat in their respective churches 'promiscuouslie with the rest of the auditorie; which looses mutche of the honour and dignitie of the universities. . .'. He insisted that they should sit, instead, in 'fitt and convenient places within the quires' and that they should 'use the . . . habit of gownes, according to thair degrees, in schooles, universitie, and streetes'.[3]

The college laws issued by Principal William Guild in 1641 reinforced the idea of seclusion. Students could not leave the college without permission and were to return as soon as possible, shunning evil company. They were to go in a body to church and to games, their dress and demeanour closely regulated, their games afternoons beginning and ending with roll calls. These laws were re-issued at intervals in the course of the century, reinforced where they had proved to be defective and amended to suit changing circumstances: in 1686, for example, Principal George Middleton reaffirmed the long-standing prohibition against wandering at night, banning the students not only from the Old Town but from the New.[4]

The magistrates of Old Aberdeen co-operated with the college to keep the students out of trouble. In 1605 a joint session of the bailies and the college staff decreed that no brewer should sell students food or drink. In 1612 the council forbade townsfolk to lend them more than a merk; and in 1613 it banished a couple who had seduced them from their studies. Some restrictions bore repeating: in 1691 the council decreed that students should not be served drinks after 8 p.m.[5]

College laws and council regulations proved ineffective as the century progressed. Student numbers rose from around sixty in the early decades to twice that figure in the second half. The students themselves ranged from boys of fourteen or less to young men of eighteen or more.[6] They were by nature, according to one of their professors, both ardent and impulsive.[7] So it is hardly surprising that they evaded the restrictions imposed by the staff and succumbed to such temptations as were on offer. Just how often they did it and how far they went, is difficult to say. The number of recorded offences is, admittedly, small; revisions of the college laws, however, and reports of college visitations suggest that these lapses may have been excessive but were by no means exceptional.

Students who lived in clearly had no problems getting out and into trouble. Royal commissioners, inspecting the college in 1676, ordered the masters to attend to 'the keeping of the colledge gates both night and day' but complained the following year that disorders were still increasing. Not that indiscipline of this sort was confined to King's: the Parliamentary Commission of 1695 ordered students at all the universities to wear their red gowns, 'that therby vaging [idle strolling] and vice may be discouraged'. At King's the effect of this injunction – if, indeed, it had any – soon wore off: in 1700 Principal Middleton had to issue a 'severe reproof' to the bursars for not wearing their gowns and for truancy.[8]

A growing number of students lodged in the town, preferring a bed there to the dilapidated, overcrowded and expensive rooms in the south wing of King's. There are a few, brief references to the arrangements: in 1659 James Ogilvie from Cullen lodged alone, his classmate, Francis Ruthven from Kincardineshire, shared his quarters with several others, and at least two students lived with the college porter; in 1709 Alexander Bain from Foveran had his

9. King's College about 1670.

own room in the house of James Lillie, a merchant.[9] Students in lodgings were bound by the same laws as those living in college. They kept college hours, beginning their studies around seven, leaving at nine for breakfast and at noon for dinner; they supped at seven o'clock, returning, when the bell rang at eight, for a further hour of study.[10] Thereafter they were unsupervised: which is, presumably, how Alexander Bain, in the privacy of his own room, came to father a child on James Lillie's servant.

Students on the loose were a source of irritation, sometimes alarm, to the townsfolk. In 1668, for example, some students uttered 'certaine speiches' against John Fraser, a local landowner, and his wife; the incident turned ugly when Fraser 'did pluck and tugg' their ringleader and threatened 'to put ane puinyard [dagger] through his cheicks.' Fraser made a similar threat to the subprincipal, claiming that he had lost control of his charges, and was sent to cool off in prison. In 1689 Alexander Stead was asked to tell the kirk session how he came to be in a married woman's bedroom; he explained that, being chased by some students between nine and eleven o'clock at night, he had taken refuge in her house and, when they forced the door open, had hidden under her bed.[11] Admittedly, the aggro was not all one way. Town children peed at the college gate, if the porter did not stop them; on one occasion, at least, boys broke into the college during the vacation; and in 1701 Anne Mitchell was punished by the council for wounding a second-year student, John Milne.[12]

Students could be hard on property. In 1700, for example, they held a disorderly meeting in St Machar's and broke a door. In 1705 they broke down another door, this time of the tolbooth, in order to free a prisoner.[13] Even when they relaxed on the bowling green in front of the college, they were still a problem. In 1663 the kirk session disapproved of them 'playing at the bullets because it was dangerous and there had bein skaith [harm] gottin that way'; and in 1668 the town council complained of their games of 'bulleis' and 'off divers and sundrie inconveinents that have fallen out therby'.[14]

Bitterness between the staff of King's and Marischal was a further source of trouble, erupting into violence between students on the streets. A notorious instance in Old Aberdeen, the 'riot' of 1659, has been described elsewhere. Most of the subsequent skirmishes took place in the New Town; but there was a further 'tumult' in Old Aberdeen during the session of 1700/1, when King's was said to be 'in ane uproar'. The circumstances are obscure, but some of the townsfolk were caught up in the affair and were taken to court.[15]

Politics, too, could bring the students out. At the beginning of 1716, four of them held a meeting in the main classroom of the college. They made speeches, in Latin, 'reflecting on the king and his generals and in commendation of the Pretender'. Then they went out and attacked the minister's house and that of Alexander Taylor of Cotton, robbing the latter of his weapons. In February seven students, most of them armed (courtesy, perhaps, of Alexander Taylor), made the porter ring the college bells and forced William Walker, the elderly town drummer, to march through the streets, 'desiring all persons to come and see the duke of Brunswick [i.e. George I] in effigy committed to flames'. They carried a picture of the king mounted on a musket and ordered Walker to burn it on a bonfire at the college gate. Walker demurred, the wind blew the picture away and a student burned it instead. The demonstrators were subsequently expelled, although Principal Middleton and two regents, Jacobite sympathisers, carefully absented themselves from the hearing.[16]

These breaches of discipline fell to a large extent within the jurisdiction of the college. Students accused of sexual offences answered to a different authority – the kirk session. In the period 1620–1720 it investigated eighteen such cases; nine took place in the 1670s, the decade during which royal commissioners commented adversely on the indiscipline at King's. Six were of fornication (sexual intercourse) and six more involved accusations of paternity. The remaining six were of behaviour that had caused a scandal: in 1677, for example, John Stewart was found in a house, drunk at the fireside, his posture suggesting to a witness that he might have had sex with a woman there.[17]

Most of the cases involved a single student. The drunken John Stewart, however, was accompanied by a more active classmate, and a case of 1673 involved three or four.[18] The youngest offender was William Gordon, accused in 1648 of fathering a child although, as the session sceptically observed, he was 'bot ane bairne at the gramer scoole'; by the time the accusation was under investigation, however, he was in his first year at King's.[19] There was one other first-year student, two in their second year and three each in their third and fourth. Another student, William Cumming, was 'scarcely sixteen' and had not reached his final year when he fathered a child in 1697.[20] Some offenders were from the neighbourhood of Old Aberdeen: William Gordon came from Kethocksmill, John Sandilands from Craibstone. Others came from much further afield: James Wood, from St Vigeans, in Angus; William Cumming, from Inverness.[21] Gordon, Sandilands and Wood were all from landed families; Gordon's father was, indeed, a prominent figure in the kirk session and council of the Old Town.[22]

In eight of the eighteen cases, the students confessed their sin, did public penance and were absolved. John Forbes, in 1643, appeared before the session one Sunday, confessed to the sin of fornication, sat on the penitent's stool before the congregation in church, and was absolved the same day. Five more were, like him, first offenders; but the other two had sinned previously, elsewhere. Alexander Bain, for example, who fathered a child in his lodgings, had been convicted of fornication in the parish of Slains at the age of fifteen. He had, therefore, to appear six times as a penitent and to pay a fine of £20 before receiving absolution. One student confessed but did not go through the disciplinary procedure. This was Peter Ramsay, accused of fornication in 1677. After a year had elapsed, he wrote from his home in Crimond admitting his offence and binding himself to appear as a penitent and to pay not only his own fine but that of his partner. When, a year later, he had still failed to appear, the session discovered that he had been charged with a further offence at home. He died before the matter could be settled.[23]

Two students denied their guilt. In 1679 James Wood, back at St Vigeans, put his denial in writing; but the session and subsequently the presbytery of Aberdeen insisted that he should purge himself by oath. Eventually the presbytery in Angus persuaded him to swear, but in a form that did not satisfy their brethren in Aberdeen, who observed stiffly that they thought fit 'not to insist any more in it, for seing they have discharged themselves if the presbytery there will not take the right methodes of discipline, the blame lyes on themselves'.[24]

In the remaining cases the proceedings are either tantalisingly obscure or inconclusive. In 1672, for example, two servants confessed that they had invited Farquhar MacGillivray and some fellow-students into their master's house and that one of them had had sex with Farquhar. The principal was asked to raise the matter with his staff and report back to the session. But there are no further references to Farquhar in the minutes of the college or the session although, as the servant publicly repented and was absolved. Farquhar may well have been guilty.[25]

The kirk session showed a notable degree of leniency towards the student offenders. In 1645 James Sutherland confessed to fornication but was loath to appear three times as a penitent and thereby miss three weeks' tuition. The session was sympathetic and allowed him to make a single appearance, at which he was absolved. Presumably, a similar concession had been made in the earlier case of John Forbes. When the session finally accepted that William Gordon was, indeed, old enough to have fathered a child, it spared him the ordeal of three appearances as a penitent, 'fearing that the youth would be too sore dejactit', and reduced his sentence to a single day on the stool and a fine of five merks. This was not out of regard for William's worthy father: another of the Gordon boys was pursued at the same time with the full rigour of the law.[26]

In one case, the tolerance of the session was blatantly abused. John Sandilands was accused of fornication in 1695. He wrote to the session, confessing his offence but asking that his act of repentance might be delayed on account of his age and 'especialy being before his comerades'. The session agreed but when, three years later, John had still not appeared, it pursued him again. He secured a second deferral, this time because of unexplained circumstances involving his father. In 1700 he pleaded for a third postponement, claiming that he could not pay his fine of £40. Leaving the session with what proved to be a worthless bond for the sum, he spent the next four years in Leyden. On his return he was pursued once more, this time by the presbytery; but it was not until 1706 that he appeared on the pillar as a penitent and was absolved.[27] In terms of length, Sandilands' ten years of prevarication were exceptional. Two cases, including that of the resolute James Wood, dragged on for over three years, while that of the recalcitrant Peter Ramsay lasted for over two. The majority, however, were concluded in a year or less.

The women were, in every case, the first to be reported to the session. Ten of them lived or worked in Old Aberdeen. Christian More, who had had sex with the conscientious James Sutherland, was the daughter of a smith. Janet Seaton, accused in 1673, lived with her children in a house in which students and others gathered and drank. Margaret Smart, accused in 1697, may have been the widow of a sub-porter at King's, with one son.[28] Nothing is known of Margaret Watt, who had the child of William Cumming of Inverness in the same year; but her father was literate enough to write a letter of accusation to William's family. Five were servants, like Bessie Allan, who was abused by a group of students in 1678, Elspeth Smith who was with her,[29] and Elizabeth Smith, impregnated by the lodger Alexander Bain. Again, Bessie's step-father was sufficiently literate to lodge a judicial complaint in order to clear her name. Six women, including Christian More and Margaret Watt, were first offenders; three had offended once before; a fourth committed a subsequent offence in Aberdeen, while her case was still in progress; and Janet White, who had the child of the youthful William Gordon, was (the session noted) 'bot ane drunkart'.

The perpetration of the acts is described in only a few cases. When both partners confessed their sin outright, it was not recounted at length; only when the accusations were contested or based on rumour, were witnesses called and circumstantial evidence recorded. So it is difficult to say, for example, which of the partners took the initiative. The two servants who invited Farquhar MacGillivray and his fellow-students into their house did so in a forward, not to say challenging manner; and Bessie Allan claimed that Elspeth Smith had 'brought some students . . . upon her'. In contrast, Jean Harret said in 1676 that a student 'did endeavour to defile her but she resisted him'; and Elizabeth Hay claimed in 1678 that she met a group of students, one of whom 'came to her and did cast her over'.[30]

Details of time and place are equally hard to come by. Several of the offences took place in private houses; Bessie Allan, however, was abused in a barn, where she had gone to cast malt. Others occurred out of doors: Jean Harret was assaulted on the bank of Powis Burn; Margaret Sangster, in 1693, on the road from Aberdeen;[31] Elizabeth Hay encountered her students at the side of the minister's glebe; while Bessie Allan claimed that she saw Elspeth Smith with students on the rigs at the back of the town. Most of the events occurred at night: in Bessie Allan's case around 9 p.m. Jean Harret's assailant, however, had been reading on the bank of the burn, so the incident must have happened before dark. There are some indications that the women were forced. The student who assaulted Jean Harret was said by witnesses to have plucked her down on the grass by the foot or apron. When Margaret Sangster asked the name of her partner, he threatened to strike her. Elizabeth Hay said a student had 'cast her over'; Bessie Allan that she was 'tugled and abuised'. Although some of the incidents took place in front of witnesses, on only one occasion were the offenders caught in the act by the authorities. Principal Middleton described to the session how 'on night . . . being desyrd to com into [Janet Seaton's] houss, he did find 3 students there quho quhen they heard off him, did put out the candel . . .'. Someone must have relit it, because he went on to report that 'two off them he found standing up in beds'.[32]

There is little to show what effect an appearance before the kirk session had upon students. John Sandilands' reluctance to make his repentance in front of his comrades suggests a degree of embarrassment. James Sutherland's plea for leniency shows that the process interrupted their studies. But James nonetheless went on to graduate, as did two others, including the drunken John Stewart.[33] Only in the case of William Cumming of Inverness, who impregnated Margaret Watt, is the outcome described at length. William's father had intended that he should stay at college for the full four years; that was before he heard from Margaret's father. Such a surprising letter, he said, made him alter his thoughts and dispose of William otherwise, in sending him 'to the latron' (lectern, i.e. into the legal profession). William was despatched abroad for two years; on his return, he begged the session to absolve him immediately, as he was going to work for an advocate in Edinburgh. The session, noting that he had been scarcely sixteen 'when he fell into that snare' and that he had come voluntarily, 'professing his sorrow and purpose to lead a new lyfe', showed yet again its capacity for leniency and complied.

In the course of the eighteenth century, the staff of King's tried to reverse the drift towards non-residence, partly to reassert the principle of seclusion, partly to preserve the income from chamber mails (i.e. the fees for college rooms). In 1700 they decreed that all students able to pay the fee should live in, except those whose homes were in the town; those who insisted on living out were to pay half a crown for the privilege. By 1730 they had rebuilt the residential south wing and had lowered its rates to compete with the cost of lodgings.[34] Nevertheless, students continued to prefer the town, where they were less restricted. They were also less secure: there were fights with apprentices – the town officer was called to one in 1737; and attacks by even younger assailants – a student was badly hurt when a boy threw a stone at him in 1742.[35]

In 1753 the staff tried again to enforce residence, this time as part of a major initiative to reform teaching, discipline, management and funding. They produced a battery of arguments against students living out: 'they being by that means less under the eye and authority of the masters, having less access to their assistance, and that of their fellow-students, in the prosecution of their studies, being exposed to many temptations from low or bad company, being moreover for the most part badly accommodated both in lodging and diet, and losing a considerable part of their time in going and returning to their lodgings . . .' New regulations decreed that all students should live and eat in college, although these were later amended, at the request of the local gentry, to permit their sons to board with the staff. As a result, Thomas Reid, a leading reformer, could write with satisfaction: 'we need not but look out at our windows to see when they rise and when they go to bed'.[36]

The scheme backfired. For the next five years the staff watched in dismay as numbers fell sharply in comparison with those of Marischal. Some attributed the decline directly to the new rules, but Reid laid the blame elsewhere. Marischal, he said, had benefited from the prosperity and growing population of the New Town: 'Our Old Town has none of these advantages and is become a desolate country village.' This bleak view of Old Aberdeen was evidently shared by the students.[37] Rules made in 1765 show that they were increasingly attracted to the New Town, not least by its book-auctions. The harbour was another attraction, and it was there, in 1770, that a party of students fell foul of some sailors, who pursued them back to King's and laid siege to the college.[38]

The perils of living in and living out, and the pull of the New Town over the Old, are breezily described by the actor-manager George Colman, banished from idle dissipation in Oxford to the austerity of Old Aberdeen in 1781. George spent over a week in lodgings, while his unpapered, unfurnished college room was made ready. He lived in a 'cabin, one story high, opposite to the college gate', in the care of Mrs 'Lucky' Lowe, probably the 'Mrs Lowe' who was then the college economist, or housekeeper. Although she continued to cook for him once he had moved into the college, her skill was limited and he frequently ate elsewhere. On one occasion, at least, he was invited out to dine in Old Aberdeen; but he preferred the taverns of the New Town, even though he and his friends were several times attacked on their way back by a gang of louts.[39]

By the beginning of the nineteenth century the concept of a residential college, and with it the principle of seclusion, had to all intents and purposes been abandoned. Wealthy students continued to live in what was then called the college boarding-house, paying £6 a quarter; 'a very few' were still in residence in 1825. The rest were mostly in lodgings at around half that rate.[40] Several students have left accounts of their accommodation in the Old Town. John Kennedy from Inverness, for example, entered the class of 1828 and lodged in College Bounds. The Misses Beverlay at Number 26 charged him £3.10s. a session, cleaned his shoes for 5s. extra and cooked his meal, his meat and his potatoes for 1s. a week. He found them honest, he wrote, and 'very kind to me, and I may sit at their fire and read my book as long as I please.' He does not say if other students shared his lodgings, but three years later his brother James also lodged in College Bounds, 'in a little house where there were five or six students, with two in each room and that room so small that I wonder how health was maintained'.[41]

As numbers rose, and pressure on beds in the Old Town increased, a growing number of students sought accommodation elsewhere. In the session 1854/5, when the college began to keep a register of addresses, over half of the 217 students in the four arts classes lived in the city. There were 68 in Old Aberdeen, most of them in College Bounds, the High Street and Orchard

Cottage; a further 18 stayed in the Spital. The 36 who lodged in College Bounds were crammed into nine houses: at Number 26, the Misses Beverlay had been replaced by the Misses Taylor and Gaven, with three students in their charge; at Number 25, eight shared the premises of James Smith, grocer. There is no sign that students of the same year or home town shared the same lodgings: at Number 26, for example, one student was in his first year and two in their second; they came from Forres, Cruden and Tobermory. Brothers generally stayed together, however; two from the manse at Alves lodged at Number 25, together with four students from Aberdeenshire, one from Perthshire and one from Banff.[42]

The classic account of student life at King's in the decade preceding the fusion of the two colleges is Neil Maclean's *Life at a Northern University*.[43] Maclean attended King's from 1853 to 1857, lodging for three years in George Street before moving to the Spital.[44] As a result, many of his scenes have city settings – his own rooms, those of his friends in Park Place and Charlotte Street, and in the 'Cafe Royal' or Lemon Tree in Huxter Row. The episodes set in the Old Town depict for the most part what Maclean called 'larks': students ringing doorbells, stealing doorknockers, switching shop-signs, 'pinning' carts (i.e. removing their wheels) and overturning them. Sometimes the larks turned sour. Maclean was present when a student assaulted an elderly drunk and the townsfolk came to the old man's defence. He witnessed, too, the aftermath of a spirited snowball fight, when students smashed the windows of an old woman's house. In both cases, he insists, the offenders were perceived by their fellow-students as having overstepped an accepted limit: the drunk-basher was despised as 'a dastardly wretch';[45] the window-breakers were shamed into paying for the damage.

Larks, then, were governed by a code. So, too, was the use of violence. Maclean condemns the drunk-bashing incident which brought the town out against the students, but he writes with pride and evident pleasure of the students' response: 'Blows were given and received, *thuds* such as one only hears given by man to man, sharp raps of sticks by no means light or fragile were borne on the clear air, showing that the "light and joyous sport" was progressing favourably.' He presents the snowball-fight almost as a rite of passage: 'My dear fellow', his cousin tells him, 'you

10. King's College and the High Street in 1840.

must bear with it. We all had to bear it in the days of our Bageantdom, and so must you.'[46] Maclean also describes how his friends planned an attack on a gang of thimbleriggers (i.e. street gamblers), who had fleeced one of their Highland classmates; he remarks that the townsfolk, and even the police, encouraged them, as they pelted the hustlers with stones. Thus, over a period of fifty years, as seclusion had been replaced by diaspora, so restrictions had been replaced by self-regulation according to simple concepts of honour, loyalty and decency. Maclean's book can be read as a vindication, indeed, as a celebration of the new system.

At the beginning of the seventeenth century, the staff of King's not only imposed seclusion upon their students but were themselves secluded: the New Foundation, of the 1580s, forbade them to hold public office. In the course of the century, however, they came to participate actively in the affairs of Old Aberdeen, as members of a corporation and as individuals.

As a corporate body, the staff administered the college's extensive property in the town: they collected rents and feuduties, set tacks [leases], built dykes, planted trees and, as they rebuilt and extended the college itself, gradually transformed the appearance of the southern end of the town. In addition, they nominated the ministers of St Machar's and, in the early decades at least, exercised jurisdiction over College Bounds.[47] Corporately, too, they employed townsfolk and brought business to the town's tradesmen. In 1696, for example, three college employees are mentioned in the 'List of Pollable Persons': the steward, the cook and the porter;[48] a fourth, not listed, was the college officer. In addition, four men, described in the list as 'indwellers', were paid for 'services about the college'. Among local tradesmen patronised that year were an armourer, a blacksmith, a bookbinder, a capmaker, a clockmaker, two masons, a shoemaker, a slater and a wright, together with the French jeweller and goldsmith, Stephen Agate.[49]

As individuals, members of the college devoted considerable time and effort to the town's affairs. There are several notable examples: John Lundie, regent and humanist, who served as a bailie of the town until 1644 and as an elder of the church until

1652;[50] or George Chalmers, who became principal in 1717, secured a new charter for the town the following year, and, ten years after that, was chosen to be minister of St Machar's, doubling as principal and pastor until he died in 1746.[51] A little lower in profile, but no less assiduous in their service to the community, were the father and son, George and Thomas Gordon.

In October 1706 the kirk session of St Machar's decided it needed additional elders. It recruited a merchant, a glover, a blacksmith, three farmers and George Gordon, professor of oriental languages at King's. 'Oriental languages' meant, in fact, Hebrew: he had taught it, as his father before him, for the past thirteen years.[52] George was the most eminent of the recruits and, early in December, he was elected by the session as Master of the Kirkwork, with responsibility for the fabric of the church and the revenue for its upkeep. He made conditions 'in regard', he said, 'of his many and necessary diversions'; but he accepted the post. When he failed to turn up to be admitted to office, the session clearly wondered if it had made the right choice; it need not have worried.

In January George was involved in efforts to suppress papist meetings in the parish. In February he secured the payment of an annuity owed to the church. In May, plagued by boys who broke windows and climbed up to the bells, and beasts that damaged graves, he improved the security of the church and churchyard. In June he was faced with a crisis: a pointing job on the finials of the church proved more complicated than anticipated. George did not, as he explained to the session, know much about such things, but he knew a man who did – the subprincipal of King's; with his colleague's advice he re-negotiated the contract. Soon afterwards, however, money for the work ran out and he had to arrange for a temporary subvention from the poor fund, in order to pay the workmen. George had other, routine tasks to perform: he audited his predecessor's accounts, sat in on several cases of fornication – one of them consummated at the back of King's, though not by a student – and represented the session at the provincial synod. The session met 54 times that year; George was present on 36. In addition, he went to at least seven other meetings, to inspect the fabric, for example, and deal with contractors. Such diligence evidently stilled the session's early doubts about his commitment. On 30 November he was re-elected to the post.

In 1714 George had a son, who was destined to become one of the best known 'characters' of the college in an age when it was, if anything, over-endowed with them. Thomas Gordon held office as regent and humanist for 65 years until his death in 1797. He was heavily involved in the constitutional wrangles of the 1760s, compiled the first comprehensive history of the college (for the Old Statistical Account), acquired a reputation for pedantry but was nevertheless remembered fondly by generations of students to whom he and his sisters served tea, toast and cake in Humanity Manse.[53] He was also, from 1750–55, a bailie of Old Aberdeen.[54]

Thomas was elected in October 1749. He sat through a meeting devoted to routine business – the inspection of weights and measures, the policing of the market, the cleansing of the street, the raising of the town officer's wages so that he could buy shoes and stockings – before making his acceptance. He presided over his first meeting the following January and, at his second, was embroiled in controversy. The council proposed to pave the road from the market cross to the church, funding the work from voluntary contributions, which Thomas was asked to organise. But the townsfolk refused to contribute, and in May the work came to an ignominious stop; only when the council had a windfall in July, was it resumed. The following year was quiet, but in 1752 Thomas presided over meetings which resolved to suppress begging, appointed a second town officer for this purpose, and embarked on further municipal improvements. Two more years of routine followed, then in 1755 there was a further flurry of activity: as senior bailie, Thomas took on – and ultimately saw off – the Commissioners of Supply over the repair of the town's streets. The last meeting at which he presided attempted to resolve a conflict at St Machar's, caused by innovations in the singing of psalms. If anything, it made the situation worse and led to the celebrated case in the Court of Session between Gideon Duncan, a truculent weaver who defended the old ways, and the Senatus of King's, which found itself in the unaccustomed position of promoting the new.[55]

Members of the college, like George and Thomas Gordon,

took part in the town's business as members of the community. The townsfolk, in turn, regarded them as neighbours, without undue reverence. The seventeenth-century sub-principal who was threatened with 'ane puinyard', was also reported to the kirk session for swearing, playing cards and associating with papists.[56] A sub-principal of the eighteenth century was treated with open ridicule. This was Roderick Macleod, who held office as regent, sub-principal and principal for 67 years. George Colman recounts how, after many years as a thrifty bachelor, with the college porter to oil his boots and rub down his pony, and a maid-of-all-work to make his bed and his barley-broth, Macleod took a young wife. Immediately, he had his shabby manse repainted, hired a footman and a lady's maid, had his clothes cleaned – he reckoned to change his linen twice a week – and bought a new suit for the wedding. All this, as his neighbours watched with glee.[57] A nineteenth-century incumbent of the sub-principal's manse, Hugh Macpherson, was shown more respect. Unpublished correspondence from Macpherson, his wife and daughters to two sons abroad suggests why: it is suffused with affection and good humour, placidly retailing news of the college and gossip of the town. In November 1837 the family is planting roots and bringing in the geraniums; in March 1838 the youngsters go to the circus to see the equestrian, Ducrow; in April 1838 they entertain the Forbeses of Blelack, whose brother 'has turned very old-looking, with plenty of whiskers'; in May they report that 'the singing in the old town church is improved lately, chiefly owing, it is said, to the removal of Nelly Rae, by marriage, from the choir'.[58]

During the nineteenth century, Macpherson and his colleagues at King's continued to hold municipal office. As the town grew ever more sedate and somnolent, however, it seems likely that this occupied less of their time than before, and that they devoted themselves increasingly to academic business – responding, resisting and ultimately resigning themselves to the proposals of successive university commissions for union with Marischal. The town itself viewed any change in the status of King's with alarm. Forgotten were the confrontations with the students, the tumults, the skaith, the abusings and the tuglings. The scheme of 1786, it had cried, 'would greatly reduce the value of the whole property of its inhabitants.' The scheme of 1835, it denounced as 'a public calamity'. By 1854, however, realising that some form of union was inevitable, it set out to sell itself, its sedateness and its somnolence, as well as it could. 'Old Aberdeen', the council declared, 'is from its quiet and retired situation the best place for the classes in Arts.'[59]

REFERENCES

1. The charter of 1514 was not published until 1529. L.J. Macfarlane, *William Elphinstone and the kingdom of Scotland, 1431–1514: the struggle for order* (Aberdeen, 1985), 385–7.

2. D. Stevenson, *King's College, Aberdeen, 1560–1641: from Protestant reformation to Covenanting revolution* (Aberdeen, 1990), 57 (hereafter Stevenson, *King's College*).

3. C. Innes, ed., *Fasti Aberdonenses. Selections from the records of the University and King's College of Aberdeen*, Spalding Club (Aberdeen, 1841), 393–4 (hereafter Innes, *Fasti*); Stevenson, *King's College*, 73–4.

4. Innes, *Fasti*, 225–55; Aberdeen University Library (hereafter AUL), MS K 130.

5. A.M. Munro, *Records of Old Aberdeen, 1157–1891*, New Spalding Club, 2 vols (Aberdeen, 1899–1909), i, 38, 52, 156 (hereafter Munro, *Old Aberdeen*).

6. The numbers are approximations, based on P.J. Anderson, ed., *Roll of alumni in arts of the University and King's College of Aberdeen, 1596–1860*, Aberdeen University Studies 1 (Aberdeen, 1900), 204–6 (hereafter Anderson, *Roll*); see also Stevenson, *King's College*, 55–6, 90. The evidence for ages is largely impressionistic.

7. W. Douglas, *Academiarum vindiciae . . .* (Aberdeen, 1659), 34.

8. Innes, *Fasti*, 342, 346, 355, 372; AUL MS K 39, 5.

9. AUL MS K 231/12/5, 7, 9; St Machar's Cathedral (hereafter SMC), Kirk Session Records, MS CH2/1020/10, 57.

10. Innes, *Fasti*, 229; AUL, MS K 130.

11. Munro, *Old Aberdeen*, i, 115–7, 216; SMC, MS CH2/1020/7, 172.

12. Innes, *Fasti*, 422; SMC, MS CH2/1020/5, 142; Aberdeen City Archives (hereafter ACA), Old Aberdeen Court Book, 1697– 1719, 70.

13. SMC, MS CH2/1020/8, 181; AUL, MS K 39, 52–3; the damage to the tolbooth is not mentioned in the council's minutes or accounts.

14. Munro, *Old Aberdeen*, i, 113; ii, 58.

15. C. A. McLaren, 'Affrichtment and riot: student violence in Aberdeen 1659–1669', *Northern Scotland*, x (1990), 1–17; Munro, *Old Aberdeen*, i, 224.

16. J. Allardyce, ed., *Historical papers relating to the Jacobite period 1699–1750*, New Spalding Club (Aberdeen, 1896), ii, 585–96.

17. SMC, MS CH2/1020/5, 227.

18. Ibid. 3, 811.

19. Ibid. 2, 295; Anderson, *Roll*, 17.

20. SMC, MS CH2/1020/8, 82.

21. Ibid. 5, 366; 8, 15.

22. AUL, Gordon of Cairnfield, MS 1164/11, 80–2.

23. SMC, MS CH2/1020/2, 80; 5, 226, 295; 6, 5, 13; 10, 68, 80–5.

24. Ibid. 6, 24, 29–30, 49, 53, 99–100.

25. Ibid. 3, 783, 785, 788.

26. Ibid. 2, 109, 112, 296, 312, 329.

27. Ibid. 8, 14, 15, 162, 196; 9, 522.

28. Ibid. 3, 811–3; 8, 67; J. Stuart, ed., *List of pollable persons within the shire of Aberdeen 1696*, 2 vols (Aberdeen, 1844), ii, 592 (hereafter Stuart, *List*).

29. SMC, CH2/1020/5, 274, 278.

30. Ibid. 190, 268.

31. Ibid. 7, 246, 248.

32. Ibid. 2, 811.

33. P. J. Anderson, ed., *Officers and graduates of University and King's College Aberdeen, 1495–1860*, New Spalding Club, (Aberdeen, 1893), 189, 210 (hereafter Anderson, *Officers*).

34. AUL, MS K 39, 19; 42, fol. 66r.

35. Munro, *Old Aberdeen*, i, 228; ACA, Old Aberdeen Court Book, 1735–84, fol. 50r.

36. *Abstract of some statutes and orders . . . 1753, with additions, 1754* (Aberdeen, [1754]), 5, 17; Letter to Archibald Dunbar, printed in *Alma Mater*, xx (1902), 62–3.

37. AUL, Letter to William Tytler, MS K 255, Box 42.

38. Ibid. K 46, fols 2v–3r; J. M. Bulloch, *History of the University of Aberdeen 1495–1895* (London, 1895), 178–9. See also W. R. Humphries, *William Ogilvie and the projected union of the colleges*, Aberdeen University Studies 117 (Aberdeen, 1940), 32.

39. G. Colman, *Random Recollections*, 2 vols (London, 1830), ii, 81–116 (hereafter Colman, *Recollections*); Anderson, *Officers*, 93.

40. W. Thom, *History of Aberdeen*, 2 vols (Aberdeen, 1811), 46; *Evidence . . . taken and received by the Commissioners . . . for*

visiting the Universities of Scotland, 4 vols (London, 1837), iv, 226–7.

41. H. A. Kennedy, *Old Highland Days* (London, [1901]), 62–3, 69–70.

42. Aberdeen Central Library, microform of Census enumerator's book, 1851, College Bounds; AUL, MS K 24, under date; *Directory for the City of Aberdeen 1854–55* (Aberdeen, 1854).

43. N. Maclean, *Life at a Northern University* (Glasgow, 1875; ed W.K. Leask, Aberdeen, 1906); references are to the 1906 edn (hereafter Maclean, *Life*).

44. Anderson, *Roll*, 181; AUL, MS K 24, under 1854/5.

45. Maclean, *Life*, 73–4.

46. Ibid. 177.

47. W. Orem, *A Description of the Chanonry, Cathedral, and King's College of Old Aberdeen, in the Years 1724 and 1725* (Aberdeen, 1791), 89 (hereafter Orem, *Description*).

48. Stuart, *List*, ii, 588, 589, 592, 593.

49. AUL, MS K 55/17, fols 18–19.

50. Anderson, *Officers*, 46–7; Munro, *Old Aberdeen*, i, 75–6; ii, 147.

51. Anderson, *Officers*, 27; Orem, *Description*, 118.

52. Anderson, *Officers*, 72. The following account is based on: SMC, MS CH2/1020/9, 589–678.

53. Anderson, *Officers*, 49, 62; A Allardyce, ed., *Scotland and Scotsmen in the eighteenth century: from the MSS of John Ramsay of Ochtertyre*, 2 vols (Edinburgh) i, 287–300; P.L. Gordon, *Personal memoirs . . .*, 2 vols (London, 1830), i, 27; D. Sage, *Memorabilia domestica . . .*, ed. D. Withrington (Edinburgh, 1975), 25.

54. The following account is based on: ACA, Old Aberdeen Council Minutes, 1738–62, 213–349.

55. M. Patrick, *Four centuries of Scottish psalmody* (Oxford, 1949), 155–9.

56. Munro, *Old Aberdeen*, ii, 44.

57. Anderson, *Officers*, 28; Colman, *Recollections*, ii, 96–7.

58. W. Walker, *Reminiscences, academic, ecclesiastic and scholastic* (Aberdeen, 1904), 23. The correspondence is in the possession of Mrs S. Smithson, who has made transcripts (AUL MS 3350) and has kindly permitted me to quote from them.

59. Munro, *Old Aberdeen*, i, 201–2, 207, 211.

Old Aberdeen – the Buildings

John S. Smith

Introduction:

Writing in 1725, William Orem, the Town Clerk of the Aulton noted that 'Old Aberdeen is a long town, irregularly built, and since the Revolution and the loss of its bishopric, having been deserted by the many considerable families who had houses round close, its principal dependence is on the college'.[1] Over one hundred years later, in the mid nineteenth century, Billings commented that 'the houses are venerable, standing generally in ancient ground; and save that the beauty and tranquility have led to the creation of a few pleasant modern villas dotting it here and there, whoever treads the one echoing street of the Aulton for the first time, feels that two centuries must have brought very little external change'.[2] Old Aberdeen in Billings time was mainly inhabited by academics, divines and some overwintering county families. Almost three decades earlier, Kennedy believed that 'Old Aberdeen possesses many advantages as a place of residence, many people of fortune, besides the members of the college, have chosen it as a place of residence'.[3] Much earlier in the mid seventeenth century, James Gordon summarised its character as 'rather a country village or market town than a citie'.[4]

These four simple statements – spanning the seventeenth, eighteenth and nineteenth centuries – identify a number of threads in the historical evolution of the Aulton, elements of which survive in tangible form today in its layout and place names, but principally in the built environment. As indicated by Grant Simpson,[5] the basic framework was established in medieval times, controlled in part by the immediate physical setting – starting with the bizarre behaviour of the course of the lower Don downstream of Gordon Mills with its great bend which Machar sought in choosing a site for his kirk, the gorge at Balgownie which offered a crossing point for the construction of a bridge in the fourteenth century and an estuary with limited possibilities for entry of small boats. To the east, lay a stretch of benty links, exposed to the North Sea coast, backed by a slight ridge of higher ground, broken through by both the Don and by the Powis Burn, the latter eventually draining into an area of raised lagoonal clays, which led to its being re-named the Tile Burn in its lower course. Exploitation of these clays was latterly to leave a distinctive imprint on the Aulton's architecture. Landwards of the ridge of higher ground, a long inland coastal slope running up towards Hilton, was drained by streams, whose waters created marshy areas and lochs, notably the loch of Old Aberdeen. In the vicinity were isolated hillocks of sand and gravel – the Spital, the Kettle Hill, the site of the Hermitage and others. These sand and gravel hillocks are clearly depicted on James Gordon's map of 1661.[6]

Three major nuclei were to develop along the natural routeway offered by the slightly raised ground between the benty links and the inland coastal slope – now the High Street-Don Street axis; from north to south respectively the Chanonry – the *ecclesiastical quarter* serving the cathedral, the High Street (and a part of Don Street) forming the *merchantile quarter*, and the College quadrangle on College Bounds – the *academic quarter*.[7] These quarters still retain today the focal and visually striking buildings of Cathedral, Town House and King's College Crown Tower, all standing in relatively open space. For this in itself, we should be grateful! Subsequently the unity of Aulton was to be isolated by King Street, respected by Bedford Road, but violated by St Machar Drive in the 1920s. A further minor nucleation with a distinctive historic and architectural parentage developed around the Brig of Balgownie – the group of buildings at either end of the bridge known as Netherdon and Cot Town. This essay attempts to set the Aulton's buildings, including some of those no longer with us, into their historical, socio-economic and architectural contexts, drawing on cartographic, documentary and pictorial sources of information. For ease of description, the buildings are examined in the context of the four nuclei identified above.

The ecclesiastical quarter: the Chanonry

The christian connection begins in the late sixth century AD with the tradition of a Celtic foundation by Machar on a site where a river approaching the sea takes the curve appropriate to a crozier. No trace of this building survives, but the Celtic cross-slab, found in a dyke in the Chanonry, and re-erected at the north-east exit from King's College quadrangle, seems likely to relate to this period. In 1131–2 bishop Nectan of Mortlach was translated to Aberdon under the aegis of David I. The initial bishopric at Mortlach had been founded by Malcolm II, in recognition of having 'ramscuttered' the Danes near old Mortlach Church in 1010. In accordance with his pre-battle vow, he extended the church there by three spears' lengths! – a legend which also seems to occur at Monymusk in connection with the Norman tower. A modest building of Cathedral status overlooking the Don on the present site may be presumed, and indeed a fragment of the masonry survives in the Cathedral charter room.[8] According to Hector Boece, some renovations to this first building took place towards the end of the thirteenth century and into the early fourteenth century, at around the same time as the completion of the Bridge of Balgownie (1329).[9] The Cathedral records of the period suggest a chapter of thirteen canons, thus perhaps indirectly confirming the need for extra space.[10] However the seeds of the present Cathedral fabric were sown towards the end of the fourteenth century – under Kinninmund and Lichton – with the erection of the granite nave and martial west front, the former incorporating at the east end, parts of a sandstone central tower. The work was pushed on further in the fifteenth and early sixteenth centuries, notably Elphinstone's belfry and spire to the central tower, a new choir at the eastern end, and Gavin Dunbar's superb heraldic ceiling, with all that its content implies.[11] It was Dunbar who replaced the cap houses of the stern western towers with sandstone steeples. It may be presumed that the early masons working under Lichton's direction were more familiar in building castles than cathedrals. Thus over a span of around a century and a half, the cruciform layout was completed. Sadly the great central tower was to collapse in the late seventeenth century, mutilating the transepts and eastern nave, and from 1690, the truncated Cathedral began its life as a parish church.

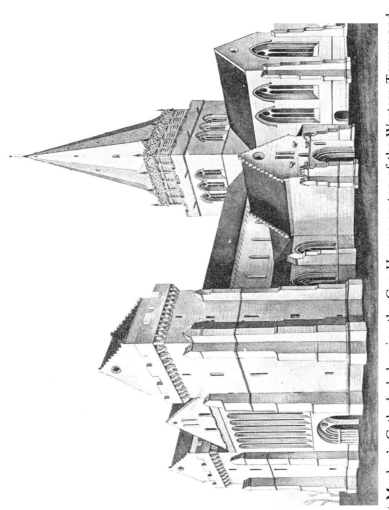

St Machar's Cathedral showing the Cap Houses on top of the Western Towers and Elphinstone's Steeple.

The community of divines which served the Cathedral resided in the Chanonry – the place of the canons – an area which had then, as today a degree of cohesion and individuality, derived from its layout, and in the days of the divines, from its four entrances – Cluny's, Tillydrone, the Bishop's Gate and Chaplain's Court. The Bishop's residence, dignified as a palace, sat on the ground now occupied by Dunbar Hall of Residence. According to James Gordon, the palace 'was large and fair; its buildings and gardings, and its quholl circuit, all enclosit with a strong wall divyding it from the neighbour buildings'.[12] In Gordon's day, scarcely a stone remained, except 'the garding'. Some of its stone had been used in the 'new worke', presumably the Square Tower in King's College quadrangle, the University's first custom built student residence. The layout of the palace appears to have been quadrangular, with corner towers surrounding a central courtyard. The summer house in the garden was three storeys high, ensuring a good seaview! There were the usual bake and brew houses and the essential doocot. Hector Boece, whose authority according to Orem 'is better and more to be believed' records the burning of the palace by 'the Englishmen' in 1333 – hence the need for an element of defensibility, perhaps more cosmetic than real, in both palace and Chanonry layout.[13] To the south of the palace garden stood the Chaplain's Court, which from Orem's description, also appears to have been set around a courtyard, with accommodation for 20 canons, and including a music and song school. Of the original elements of the complex, only the moulded arch of a pend remains, surmounted by the arms of Gavin Dunbar. The site is now occupied by a crow-stepped 3 storey house of seventeenth century origins. Also near to the bishops' garden and Cathedral stood Dunbar's Hospital, a church-inspired Old Folk's Home carrying the name of its founder, and provided with a charter signed by James V in 1536. It was designed for accommodating 12 poor men of the burgh in single rooms, with a common kitchen and the obligatory oratory. It was already ruinous by the eighteenth century, having been replaced in its *raison d'etre* by the Bede House in 1676. Other individual buildings dating back to the heyday of the medieval cathedral community, and both shown on Gordon's map as ruinous, were the Leper House (on

12. Chaplain's Court, The Chanonry.

the east side of Kings Crescent), sitting in no-mans land between
Old and New Aberdeen, and the Spital Church and hospital,
dedicated to St Peter, and founded in the mid twelfth century by
Kininmund. The arrangement of medieval manses and their
gardens is best shown pictorially on Gordon's map. He
describes most of them as then 'ruinous' with the notable
exception of the one standing nearest to the Cluny Port which
was, in his day, 'laitlie enlarged by the additione of a brave
gallerie, adorned with a varietie of paynting, as also with a
gairding, the goodliest and the greatest in Aberdeen' by the
industry of Sir Alexander Gordon of Cluny around 1622.[14]
Orem's text gives several examples of the fate of the canons'
lodgings and grounds – bought up by the nobility or the
academics for redevelopment and letting. Writing of the manse
originally the property for the Parson of Kincardine O'Neil
which stood on the west side of the Chanonry, Orem relates that
'the great lodging pertained lately to Mr Alexander Fraser of
Powis, sub-principal of King's College 'who demolished it, and
with the stones therof, built his malt-burn at Powis Burn, near
his own house, and disposed of the glebe to the present
proprietor George Connon in 1712'. The same academic entrepreneur, Alexander Fraser bought from William Anderson, a
house on the west side of the High Street 'almost opposite to the
College gate, with a little yard, and some back short riggs at the
end therof . . . all the rest of the ground being "deep sinking
mire"'.[15] Fraser built two great and three lesser houses on the
side of the Powis Burn, and made out four yards planted with
trees around about their dikes' – the said houses and yards
paying him yearly 500 merks! Orem again provides a hint as to
the Chanonry social profile in the seventeenth century – the
Deanery with its revenue is appropriated to the minister of St
Machar – but 'the houses of the other prebends were mostly
taken down about 1725 – these houses were mostly on the west
and north side of the Chanonry, as on the east were houses of
the principal nobility, particularly the Duke of Gordon'.[16] Old
Aberdeen was already fulfilling the role of a town residence for
county families. Although the contemporary dykes and land
plots reflect the basic outlines of the medieval ecclesiastical
quarter with some very substantial amalgamation (for example
Chanonry Lodge appears to occupy with its grounds at least

13. The Bede House, Don Street.

three medieval manse sites), the majority of the houses lining the
Chanonry today are late eighteenth or early nineteenth century
in date, mainly two storey, basement and attic. Many of them
have chimneys or even extension wings of brick. No.8,
Chanonry is a classy Palladian-style mansion, while No.9,
Mitchell's Hospital (1801) is an attractive 3-sided building with
central gable and bellcote, originally designed to accommodate
'five widows and five unmarried daughters of merchant and
trade burgesses of Old Aberdeen'.

Much of the character of the Chanonry resides in its 'external
appearance' – derived from a feeling of individuality and
seclusion aroused by its high dykes, spacious grounds and
wooded character. Although the architecture is mainly of the last
two hundred years, the street plan and general aura is of the
medieval ecclesiastical precinct.

The merchantile quarter:

This part of the Aulton is represented by the southern stem of
the Y-plan, with an extension north-eastwards along Don Street
on the old highway to the Balgownie crossing. Its central spine is
pleasingly diversified by closes and lanes, and bounded to east
and west by the backbutts, represented today by Dunbar Street
and Elphinstone Road. The oldest buildings, for example,
Grant's Place of single-storeyed cottages date back to the early
eighteenth century (1720s), and the main artery of the High
Street retains the causewayed character of cassies and granite
paving slabs. It seems possible that this would have been the
style of finish appropriate to the medieval Aulton as the upkeep
of causeways is mentioned in the Burgh records.

The Aulton's charter as a burgh of barony (1489) gave the
bishops rights of mills, fishings, forests and warrens, and its
burghers enjoyed the right to buy and sell 'wines, wax, cloth
woollen and linen, broad and narrow and other merchandise' . . .
and 'to have and hold bakers, brewers, butchers and sellers of
flesh and of fish and other craftsmen'. The hereditary guardian
of Old Aberdeen was the Earl of Huntly.

The dignity of the Aulton as a separately administered burgh
is epitomised by the Town House, sitting on the highest part of

14. Mitchell's Hospital, The Chanonry.

the High Street, and carrying displayed on its walls, the sculptured arms of a previous town house of 1721. The present splendidly Georgian building (George Jaffray, 1788) is of granite with central pediment, clock tower and cupola. It looks benignly down the gradually tapering thoroughfare of the High Street, lined with gabled houses set east-west, and turns its back on the Chanonry. Some of the houses in the upper end of the High Street are grand and fashionable e.g. 81, High Street c.1780, set within ample grounds and with elegant formal approaches. The majority are however appropriately crammed, often gable-end on to the street front, presumably reflecting the original land lots designed to maximise valuable burgage frontages. Some now have entrances inserted into the street front gable, others are still entered by lanes or courts, the former offering glimpses of the old backbutts, but perhaps in medieval times serving the function of night-time cattle pends. Most houses remain of relatively simple design, but there is a definite nineteenth century social gradient in architecture from north to south. Comparison of Wood's map of 1821 and the First Edition of the Ordnance Survey large scale plans in the 1860s, confirms Billing's view, expressed in 1846, that it was fashionable to live in Old Aberdeen. The changes suggest some demolition and revamping of the eighteenth century buildings and sundry outhouses of unspecified use to provide more space around the houses, and for modest renovation. The history of the Old Tannery (No.33, High Street) is a fascinating example of the vagaries which many buildings in Old Aberdeen appear to have experienced in the eighteenth and nineteenth centuries.[17] The relative uniformity of the lower portion of the High Street in elevation and alignment can be contrasted with the mixed bag of town houses, and two-storey houses in the middle portion, and changing again to the north east, to single storey cottages in Grant's Place. One of the most distinguished of the town houses – the Dower House in Don Street at the junction with the Chanonry – is 3-storey eighteenth century with a two storey wing, built almost certainly on the site of the Cathedral Treasurer's residence.

Like Dunbar Street, Don Street is also diversified by its recently refurbished late nineteenth century granite tenements e.g. 36 and 44 Don Street.

15. The pantiled cottages of Grant's Place.

The Brig of Balgownie

A detached group of historic buildings hard by the fourteenth century Brig of Balgownie include the L-plan Chapter House, a misnomer, as the coat of arms above the arched pend leading to its courtyard confirms that the house was built in the mid-seventeenth century for George Cruickshank of Berriehill, some of the stone having been carted from the fabric of the old manse of Clatt in the Chanonry, which George had purchased. His house with easy access to the Don was designed for '-accommodating him at the time of his fishing'.[18]

The Academic quarter: King's College

The quadrangle of King's College – the historical kernel of the academic quarter – appears to have been a difficult site to develop. Although the inscription on the north side of the west door of the chapel provides a firm date for the onset of construction (2 April, 1500), it was apparently the completion of two years of drainage works and the installation of oak rafts on the initially marshy ground that permitted work to begin.[19] As the ground slopes southwards and eastwards from the present Town House towards the Powis burn, perhaps it may be deduced that there was no open space available further north, an indirect indication of an existing or anticipated take-up of street frontages. The Crowned tower of King's College Chapel was almost certainly the work of Thomas French, having clear equivalents in St Giles, Edinburgh and possibly St Michael's, Linlithgow. Both Hector Boece and W. Douglas Simpson concur in assigning an imperial character to the Crown (closed, not open), but modern scholars tend to believe that it here symbolises James IV's legitimate claim to imperial authority within Scotland, rather than a reflection of the Imperial Holy Roman Empire's dominion over medieval universities.[20]

The original quadrangle of the early sixteenth century was delimited by the chapel to the north, Great Hall to the east, the students and teachers rooms to the south, with the Crown Tower and Principal's quarters on the west front. The quadrangular layout not only provided seclusion from the outside world for

16. The Round Tower, King's College.

studies and the imposition of strict college rules, but also permitted the infant University and its treasures to be defended against attack by land or sea. The surviving southeastern Round Tower of 1525 – rubblecoursed with shotholes – retained a spire until blown down in 1715. Dunbar's 1525 domestic buildings were subsequently augmented by bishop Stewart's lean-to library adjacent to the southern wall of the chapel with classrooms below. That building survived until 1726. The tall Square Tower near the eastern end of King's College chapel – sometimes wrongly assigned to Oliver Cromwell – was built in 1658 as a residential unit for students. The building originally contained accommodation for 24 students and a billiard room, but was eventually converted to classrooms. Its stark outlines despite major internal changes over the centuries are akin to those of a simple Scottish tower house. Square, round tower and Chapel remain tangible elements in the outline of the medieval University, together with the original draw-well sited centrally within the quadrangle lawns. The relatively small scale of the sixteenth century University reflects the tiny group of bursaried students – who entered college in their early teens, and studied for a four year Masters degree. Regulations were perforce strict, with the college gates locked from sunset to sunrise, students encouraged to converse in Latin or French, and eating in the refectory (as was indeed the case within the last thirty years) in common with their teachers. During the sixteenth and seventeenth centuries, twenty students might graduate in a good year, as few as half a dozen in a bad year, such as the difficult times of the Civil Wars. By the eighteenth century with rising student numbers and limited college accommodation, mandatory university residence proved impossible, and the masters themselves had mainly moved out to occupy the manses in the Chanonry.

There were very significant changes in the quadrangle buildings during the nineteenth century. Externally, the new west frontage of the 1820s (John Smith), the new Library of 1870, and the south and east ranges (Robert Matheson) in the 1860s were grafted onto the Chapel and Square Tower. The library, occupying largely the site of Elphinstone's Great Hall, included a barrel-vaulted ceiling modelled on that of the chapel. The panel above its entrance includes the date of the College foundation 1494 (should be 1495), 1540, the date of completion

17. The north west corner of King's College Quadrangle.

18. New King's with its protruding staircase bays complete with
Gothic tracery.

of bishop Stewart's first official library abutting the southern wall of the chapel, 1726, the date of Fraser's restoration of that library, and finally 1870, the Victorian library. The latter was to be replaced by the Queen Mother Library in 1978.

Subsequent buildings east of the High Street replicate the quadrangular theme, notably the elegant New Kings (1912) and the Elphinstone Hall (1930), the latter with its cloisters (based on the bays in the nave of St Machar) and its fine pitchpine roof, the whole, forming with the chapel, a 3-sided open quadrangle bounded to the west by the High Street.[21] The Taylor Building compliments two late eighteenth century rubble tenements, one occupying the site of the Founder's Brewery – to outline an additional quadrangle. To the west of the High Street sits Powis Lodge whose eastern and western blocks (respectively 1697 – facing High Street, and 1711), the latter remodelled in 1829 by architect John Smith, provides through its early nineteenth century gateway minarets, a touch of the Turkish to old Aberdeen![22] The original builder of the 1697 Powis Lodge was Alexander Fraser, sub-principal of King's College, the academic entrepreneur (*vide supra*).

The total architectural package of Chanonry, merchantile quarter, elegant town houses and academic quarter is an appealing and historical gem, and it is to be hoped that the newly inaugurated Conference and Visitor Centre will attract even more vistors to appreciate and enjoy its many qualities.

REFERENCES

1. W. Orem, *A description of the Chanonry, Cathedral and King's College of Old Aberdeen*, 1724 – 5 (Aberdeen, 1830) 64 – 5.

2. R. W. Billings, *The Baronial and Ecclesiastical Antiquities of Scotland* Vol.1, 1846.

3. W. Kennedy, *Annals of Aberdeen* Vol.2 (Aberdeen, 1814) 309.

4. James Gordon, *A Description of both touns of Aberdeen* (Aberdeen, 1842) 21.

5. Grant Simpson, this volume.

6. James Gordon, *op.cit.*, folding map. See also p.8 this volume.

7. Grant Simpson, *Old Aberdeen in the Seventeenth Century* (Aberdeen, 1980).

8. Leslie Macfarlane, this volume.

9. Hector Boece, *Scotorum Historiae* (Paris, 1526).

10. Leslie Macfarlane, *St Machar's Cathedral and its medieval records* (Aberdeen, 1987).

11. David McRoberts, *The Heraldic Ceiling of St Machar's Cathedral* (Aberdeen, 1981).

12. James Gordon, *op.cit.*, 23.

13. Hector Boece, *op.cit.*

14. James Gordon, *op.cit.*, 22.

15. W. Orem, *op.cit.*, 209.

16. W. Orem, *op.cit.*

17. Cecily and Gordon Anderson, The Old Tannery No.33, High Street, Old Aberdeen, *Aberdeen University Review,* 41, 1966, 161–73.

18. Cuthbert Graham and Stewart Todd, *Old Aberdeen – Burgh, Cathedral and University* (Aberdeen, 1978), 4.

19. Richard Fawcett, The Architecture of King's College Chapel and Greyfriar's Church, *Aberdeen University Review*, 53, 1989, 102–26.

20. Leslie Macfarlane, *Guide to King's College* (Aberdeen, 1982), 4. For a different view, namely that the Crown symbolises the comity of European nations under Pope and Kaiser, see W. Douglas Simpson, *Guide to King's College*, (Aberdeen, 1962), 4. For further information, see L. J. Macfarlane, *William*

Elphinstone and the Kingdom of Scotland 1431–1514 (Aberdeen 1985), 330 and L. J. Macfarlane *A Visitor's Guide to King's College* (Aberdeen 1991), 2nd revised edition.

21.   William Watson, *Marshall Mackenzie: Architect in Aberdeen* (Aberdeen, 1985), 31.

22.   William A. Brogden, *Aberdeen: An illustrated architectural guide* (Aberdeen, 1986), 81–96.

Centre for Scottish Studies, University of Aberdeen
Director and Editor of Pamphlets: Dr John S. Smith (Department of Geography)
Editor of *Northern Scotland*: Professor Peter L. Payne (Department of History)
Conference Organiser: Mr A. Rodney Gunson (Department of Geography)

NORTHERN SCOTLAND is the annual journal of the Centre. Full details on
subscription, content, availability of back numbers, from the Centre.

CENTRE PAMPHLETS (in print)
(Available from bookshops, the Queen Mother Library and the Centre)
Hazel Carnegie, *Harnessing the Wind. Captain Thomas Mitchell of the Aberdeen White
  Star Line*   £2.95
D. P. Willis, *Sand and silence. Lost villages of the North*   £3.00
David Toulmin, *The Tillycorthie story*   £4.50
David Summers, *Fishing off the Knuckle. The Story of Buchan's fishing villages* £3.00
Nancy H. Miller, *Peterhead and the Edinburgh Merchant Company. Visits by the
  Governors to their Buchan estates, 1728–1987*   £3.00
James S. Wood, *For Heaven's Sake*   £3.00
W. Douglas Simpson, *Dunollie Castle and the Brooch of Lorne*   £3.95
Flora Youngson, *Dominie's Daughter*   £3.50

PUBLISHED JOINTLY BY THE CENTRE AND INSTITUTE OF TERRESTRIAL
ECOLOGY
Caring for the High Mountains. Conservation of the Cairngorms
Edited by J. W. H. Conroy, Adam Watson and A. R. Gunson   £6.00

Prices include postage. Cheques should be made payable to the Centre for Scottish
Studies.

PUBLICATIONS BY ABERDEEN UNIVERSITY PRESS
  SPONSORED BY THE CENTRE
(Available from bookshops and the Centre)
New Light on Medieval Aberdeen. Edited by John S. Smith   £4.95
Robert Barclay, *Reminiscences of an unlettered man.* Edited by David Stevenson £4.95
From lairds to louns. Country and burgh life in Aberdeen, 1600–1800.
  Edited by David Stevenson   £4.95
Aberdeen in the nineteenth century. The making of the modern city.
  Edited by John S. Smith and David Stevenson   £4.95
Fermfolk & Fisherfolk. Rural Life in Northern Scotland.
  Edited by John S. Smith and David Stevenson   £4.95
*Covenant, Charter and Party. Traditions of Revolt and Protest in Modern Scottish
  History.* Edited by Terry Brotherstone   £9.95
Grampian Battlefields. The Historic Battles of North East Scotland from AD40 to 1745.
  By Peter Marren   £9.95
From Aberdeen to Ottawa in 1845. The Diary of Alexander Muir.
  Edited by George A. MacKenzie   £5.95
North East Castles. Castles in the landscape of North East Scotland.
  Edited by John S. Smith   £5.95
The Diary of a Canny Man 1818–1828. Adam Mackie, Farmer, Merchant and
  Innkeeper in Fyvie. Edited by David Stevenson   £6.95
Shipwrecks of North East Scotland 1444–1990. David M. Ferguson   £6.95
Old Aberdeen. Bishops, Burghers and Buildings. Edited by John S. Smith   £5.95

                                             Centre for Scottish Studies
                                                University of Aberdeen
                                               Old Aberdeen AB9 2UB
                                              Telephone 0224–272474